Believing in Nothing and Something

An Approach to Humanist Beliefs and Values

Believing in Nothing and Something

An Approach to Humanist Beliefs and Values

Geoff Heath

BOWLAND PRESS

Geoff Heath

Geoff Heath FRSA was Principal Lecturer in Counselling and Human Relations at the University of Derby. He has taught in all aspects of education from primary to higher, and has led county and regional courses in counselling, training for trainers, supervision and performance appraisal. He was for some years a visiting lecturer at Homerton College, University of Cambridge, and External Examiner for the Advanced Diploma in Counselling and Careers Guidance at that university. He is currently a freelance academic and writer.

Geoff Heath's other publications include:

1989   *Staff Development, Supervision and Performance Appraisal* (London, Longman).
1997   'Language and Victims' in *Responding to Disaster: The Human Aspects* (Professional Issues Group, Emergency Planning Society).
2000   'A constructivist attempts to talk to the field', *The International Journal of Psychotherapy*, Vol. 5, No. 1, 11–35.
2002a   'Philosophy and Psychotherapy: Conflict or Co-operation?', *The International Journal of Psychotherapy*, Vol. 7, No. 1, 13–52.
2002b   'Does a Theory of Mind Matter? The myth of totalitarian scientism', *The International Journal of Psychotherapy*, Vol. 7, No. 3, 185–220.

First published 2003 by
BOWLAND PRESS
PO Box 446, Chesterfield, S42 7LZ

www.bowlandpress.com

©2003 Geoff Heath

British Library Cataloguing-in-Publication Data
A British Library CIP Record is available

ISBN 0-9544221-0-4
Typeset in Minion by BBR Solutions Ltd, Chesterfield
Printed by Alden Group Ltd, Oxford

Contents

1   Preface

11   Introduction

15   On beliefs and orthodoxy

37   My approach to nihilism

51   Intimations of nihilism
      —Scientific influences
      —My sense of subjectivity

89   Believing in something
      —My approach to humanistic beliefs and values
      —The values in which I believe

117 My inconclusive conclusion

119 References

125 Index

To friends who have helped me to become clearer
about what I believe and why I might believe it.

They have also supported my commitment to my values –
even when these, and therefore I, have changed.

And to students who have been courteous enough
to take me seriously and who have been confident enough
to give me the benefit of their criticism.

Everything could have been otherwise,
and I may well not have been at all

My journey towards a nihilistic humanism

To-morrow, and to-morrow, and to-morrow,
Creeps this petty pace from day to day,
To the last syllable of recorded time;
And all our yesterdays have lighted fools
The way to dusty death. Out, out brief candle!
Life's but a walking shadow, a poor player,
That struts and frets his hour upon this stage, and then is heard
no more;
It is a tale told by an idiot, full of sound and fury,
Signifying nothing.   (*Macbeth*)

Nihilism stands at the door: whence comes this strangest of
guests?   (Nietzsche)

Nothing, in its various guises, has been a subject of enduring
fascination for millennia. Philosophers struggled to grasp it,
while mystics dreamed they could imagine it; scientists strove to
create it; astronomers searched in vain to locate it; logicians were
repelled by it, yet theologians yearned to conjure everything from
it; and mathematicians succeeded. Meanwhile, writers and jesters
were happy to stir up as much ado about Nothing as ever they
possibly could. Along all these pathways to the truth Nothing has
emerged as an unexpectedly pivotal something, upon which so
many of our central questions are delicately poised.
                                          (Barrow 2001: Preface, xi)

When they asked Socrates where he came from, he did not say
'From Athens', but 'From the world'.   (de Botton 2000: 135)

Joseph Brodsky, the dissident Russian poet, was put on trial.
Prosecutor: What are you?
Brodsky: I am a poet.
Prosecutor: Who put you on the list of poets?
Brodsky: Who put me on the list of human beings?

The individual person, like the species of which she is a member, is going nowhere discernible (or predictable), and nowhere in particular. But this is not so much a cause of grief as an invitation to go on inventing the future.   (Phillips 1999: 29)

Newscaster: The Church of England's Doctrine Commission has stated in its report that Hell exists as a state of total non-being.

Rev. Dr John Polkinghorne, Scientist, Theologian and President of Queen's College Cambridge and member of the Commission: Hell is a state of non-being indicating the very worst condition that a person could be in.

(ITV *Channel 4 News*, 7.20 pm, 11 January 1996)

Preface

Beliefs and values have erupted into a high level of public awareness.

9/11 occurred. To say that it changed the world is probably true but it is a rather Western point of view. Millions have died and are dying in internecine wars, in famines, as a result of disease and as a consequence of the policies on arms and trade which are adopted by the West, not least my own country. I do not wish to mitigate the horror of 9/11, but I simply make the obvious point that in the developing world similar disasters are part of daily life – and death. Their deaths are largely unknown to those of us in the West – unknown and generally unnamed and unmourned. No extended TV coverage for them. No individual memorial list for them. The deaths of these, my fellow human beings, are frequently referred to as 'collateral damage'. They were merely in the way. In the way were an estimated three to four thousand civilians in Afghanistan during the attempt to destroy al-Qaeda. More than were killed in the twin towers of the World Trade Center, but no international memorial services for them. There is a differential valuing of life and therefore a differential valuing of death (Chomsky 2002).

Post-9/11 the urgent popularity of books about Islam is indicative of many people's ignorance about one of the world's major faiths which is perceived, in the West, as a minority faith. What are Muslims' beliefs and values? What is a jihad? What leads some Muslims to take such drastic and aggressive action? Is there likely to be the 'clash of civilisations' predicted by Huntington

(1996)? Can such a clash be avoided? What do 'we' believe who are not part of any religious community? Does it matter what we believe if we are not religious? How might 'we' arrive at a reasonable, meaningful and satisfying belief/value system which does not rely on the notion of God?

And then 10/12 in Bali. And the Moscow hostages. And Mombasa. A Roman Catholic crucified by Protestant 'hardliners' in Northern Ireland. Now the war against Iraq. And so on …

Belief in a version of God seems to be behind these acts of gross and horrific tragedy. I know that it is not as simple as that, but whatever other motivations and reasons, it seems to be God in whose name these acts of violence are validated.

Unacceptable attributes of God were not the reason I ceased to believe in any form of God some years ago. The two main reasons were: first, I failed to be intellectually convinced that there was evidence for God's existence; and secondly, I came to the view that, emotionally, I did not need to believe in God.

Having said that, there is a deep and sometimes disturbing sense of loneliness in giving up belief in God. The world loses its divine sense of origin. Life loses its sense of ultimate purpose, direction and meaning. Moral decisions become ever more complex. A complexity increased by the realisation that we live in a plural society in which there is simply no consensus on the basic principles of morality, let alone consensus as to how to arrive at moral decisions and actions, be these in personal living or in relation to social, international, scientific and medical ethics. Eagleton comments:

> (Berlin) is right to see that what characterizes the moral order of modernity is our failure to agree on even the most fundamental questions. This is so flagrant a fact that we have forgotten to be surprised by it.   (2003: 229)

Deciding what to believe and what values to adopt also becomes considerably more difficult when the beliefs and values cease to be prepackaged, as it were, as an integral part of the religion in which I used to believe – Christianity.

But with this kind of loss comes a sense of liberation. A freedom to think, to be sceptical, to develop my own – and owned – sense of me as the creator of my believing and valuing.

There is also a sense of loss of belonging to a community. This loss may contribute to the individualism which is so prevalent in our largely secular and generally confused society. The more I experience myself as an individual the more I am likely to experience a sense of aloneness and aloneness is a source of confusion. Aloneness is the loss of community.

There are all sorts of losses which follow from ceasing to believe in God. Indeed I think that people's needs for external sources of purpose and an anxious avoidance of a deep sense of loss, direction and meaning in part explain why some continue to be religious believers, even fervent believers. It surprises me, as it did Montaigne (1533–92 CE), that some people believe strongly in things for which there is no evidence – other than a need to believe. Perhaps the apparent need to identify groups of 'others' as 'evil' is a form of negative group cohesion: a sense of meaning derived from 'not being them'. Perhaps otherness is negatively defined by the needs of the dominant and fearful in order to confirm their prejudices.

On the other hand I sense that some people drift out of belief in the traditional God but perhaps retain a vague sense of 'a power greater than ourselves' or, as is becoming popular, a vague sense of 'spirituality'. I am not content with vague drifts, nor do contemporary views on spirituality satisfy me. They seem to me to allow emotional needs for external meaning to replace a proper sense of scepticism and of need for evidence. They seem to be residues of the hope that there is some meaning outside us, some purpose to which we can be allied. They seem to avoid clear thinking and difficult decisions about meaning, beliefs and values. I have no regrets about giving up my belief in God but it has proved difficult to know what to believe and value in God's place.

Beliefs and related myths are the stories we tell ourselves

about our origins and our identities. Beliefs and myths are expressions of our need for meaning. Myths allow us to have imagined identities, imagined senses of belonging and imagined associations. Imagined because we do not know what the true reality is. Imagined because we can never know for sure what our own and others' realities are – or were, or will be. In some respects we live in a virtual world of our imagining.

My meaning arises from my human relatedness but, because I can never be totally secure in my relatedness, I imagine that I am more related than I am. I need to belong, and this need can get in the way of including others in my belonging: the 'others' who might threaten my sense of belonging and therefore of my identity as one who belongs; the stranger who may disturb the security of my myth of my imagined identity and of the imagined 'we'. The 'other' can also threaten my imagined reference group. As Williams puts it:

> 'Using other people to think with'; that is using them as symbols for points on your map, values in your scheme of things. When you get used to imposing meanings in this way, you silence the stranger's account of who they are; and that can mean both metaphorical and literal death.
>
> (R. Williams 2002: 67)

This book is my own response to some issues, concerns, confusions, challenges and opportunities which result from my calling myself a humanist. It is an account of my personal journey towards a nihilistic humanism.

I indicate some of the reasons for my humanistic position and of the reasons and transitions which led me to this position. In a sense my own personal journey has been a shift from believing in something (God) to believing in nothing (nihilism). But I have to believe in some form of meaning. I have values. I have my stories. I have my imaginative myths of meaning. They are the basis of my existence.

Having discussed the reasons for my transitions, I then

attempt to put my own humanistic beliefs and values into a reasonably brief and coherent form.

I draw on a range of literature which has informed and challenged my thinking. These authors have helped not only to relieve my sense of loneliness in the existential predicament, but also to become clearer as to what it is that I believe and what my own values are. I decided to attempt to clarify my beliefs and values for two main reasons: I had been asked to give a lecture on my philosophical/existential position to a multi-faith group, and because beliefs and values are at the forefront of my own and many people's thinking at this particular time.

This literature also helps me to update my ideas as to what I am, what I want to believe and what my values are. Unlike religious believing which tends to be retrospective, scripture based, traditional and static, my beliefs and values are not 'givens' arising either from religious tradition or scientific 'facts'. There are important distinctions between what 'is' and what 'ought to be'. My beliefs and values are the result of my consideration of what I think is best for me, for society and for culture generally. Whilst I agree with Pinker's (2002) view that there are some universal features of human nature, based on our biological inheritance (we are not blank slates), I also agree with Janet Radcliffe Richards that:

> For the materialist, on the other hand, there is no question
> of finding out by looking at the universe how things ought
> to be, because the universe has in itself no moral order.
>
> (2000: 263)

We are each responsible for choosing our beliefs and values.

I have received a great deal of help in my search for a clarification of my beliefs, in the ongoing struggle for my personal sense of meaning and in my articulation of my position not only by reading, but particularly through discussions with trusted friends. Always challenging, never cosily collusive and comfortable, we give ourselves permission to be constructively critical. But our friendship is enhancing, developmental, supportive. It is a safe relationship. There is a deep sense of trust in these relationships and I have increasingly come to think that trust is the essence of all good relationships. This may seem self-evidently true but it is not trivially true. It is important that I emphasise it. Without my trust in my friends I would not have been able to cope with those existential problems which I have had to face and from which I learn so much. I could even go so far as to say that significant aspects of the meaning of my life is embedded within the friendships which I have had and am still fortunate to have. Even in normal living, if I can't trust you and you can't trust me the chances of a productive relationship are slim indeed. The topic of trust was considered so significant that Onora O'Neill made it the theme of her 2002 BBC Reith Lectures.

I have never previously put my own beliefs into the form of a creed but it's an interesting task to try to be clear and brief about one's beliefs. My own credo follows. It does not having the ringing cadences of religious creeds. That is in part because traditional creeds use the word 'God' as a very pithy form of shorthand, but about which tomes have been written over millennia. My creed is not immutable but it is carefully thought out and is as brief as I can make it whilst at the same time stating what I want to say.

I believe that people are the only source of their meaning.

I believe in an embodied mind, not a mind distinct from the body.

I believe that my embodied mind arises from relatedness and does not exist independently of relationships. My sense of 'I' and my mental processes are social.

I believe that we are capable of understanding and controlling some aspects of the external world as well as some aspects of our own internal embodied world. I say 'some aspects' because I do not know how far this process of understanding and control is capable of going.

I believe that science has developed the most effective ways of providing certain kinds of understanding and therefore of control.

I believe that science is the best way we have of discovering what the world is like, and here world includes how the human body works.

I believe that science is infused with values – values as to what kinds of knowledge is sought, who is authorised and resourced to seek that knowledge, how that knowledge is sought and those to whom the benefits of the knowledge are made available. Values are also present in the deep sense that the very pursuit of knowledge is valid and valued.

I believe that gaining understanding and knowledge is a human activity of discovery by increasingly rigorous use of reason, carefully constructed methodologies and the use of technologies – plus insight, scepticism, doubt, curiosity, leaps of faith, serendipity, peer review, imagination, courage, dogged determination, a playful and critical attitude to received knowledge, conversation.

I do not believe that knowledge is revealed by any sort of divine being.

I do not believe that values are revealed by any sort of divine being.

I believe that fact and value are importantly different.

I believe that 'knowledge is power' (as did Francis Bacon (1561–1626 CE) who coined the term).

I believe that our everyday experiences of the world allow us to have some limited understanding of the world. We certainly seem to believe that we can make everyday sense of the world of things and of people. The more carefully we reflect on our experiences and the more critical we are of them, the more likely we are to be able to behave tolerantly, empathically, rationally and reasonably. The more we understand, the less dogmatic we should be about that which we understand.

I believe that the meanings which we construct, based on everyday experiences and scientific understanding (at varying degrees of low level), are not inherent in the knowledge which we accumulate. Rather these meanings are our inventions, whereas scientific knowledge is based on discovery. These meaning inventions tend to go beyond knowledge and understanding and involve the creation of myths, narratives, notions of origins and endings. These myths and meanings deal with the human condition in all its complexity. Meanings are affirmations of our significance to ourselves.

I believe that there are complex interactions between the beliefs which we hold about the world, the knowledge which we discover and the meanings which we create.

I believe in the complexity of things and therefore I believe in many approaches to knowledge. If there were only one truth, then there would only be one way of saying it. There are many things and therefore many things need to be said.

I believe that it may well be the case that there is no way in which we can arrive at ultimate, total understanding and final meaning. We could never know that we knew everything. Life, understanding and meaning are processes not arrivals. We shall never know it all – for which I am grateful, because total knowledge would be all too likely to result in total domination and total power.

I believe that people have a right to their own beliefs and values. I would prefer it if their beliefs and values did not involve the desire to kill, torture, degrade, exploit and humiliate others. I would also prefer it if their beliefs and values did not include the desire to convert others. I would prefer it if their beliefs and values could include the acceptance of the enhancing and co-operative benefits of conversation. I would prefer people to be sceptical of their beliefs rather than accept them dogmatically and uncritically.

As I was correcting the proofs of this book I read *The New York Review of Books* (16 January 2003: 15) in which there is a full page taken to publish a 'Statement of Conscience' signed by more than 30,000 people.

I was moved by this Statement and decided to quote two extracts, each relating to beliefs, and each of which adds an important political dimension to my own credo. These two belief statements are also entirely consistent with the values which I state in the final chapter of this book.

I ally myself with the following belief statements:

We believe that people and nations have the right to determine their own destiny, free from military coercion by great powers. We believe that all persons detained or prosecuted by the [government] should have the same rights of due process. We believe that questioning, criticism and dissent must be valued and protected. We understand that such rights and values are always contested and must be fought for.

We believe that people of conscience must take responsibility for what their own governments do — we must first of all oppose the injustice that is done in our own name.

Introduction

The immediate reason for preparing the lecture, of which this book is an expanded version, is that I had been invited to present my philosophical/existential position to the Multi-faith Group at the University of Derby. I had received an invitation to attend the launch of the third edition of the uniquely comprehensive survey of faiths in this country, *Religions in the UK* (2001), which is under the direction of Professor Paul Weller at the University. At the launch, a number of contributors made reference in their speeches to the validity of religious experiences and of spirituality. At the end I said to Paul that I simply did not understand what people meant by religious experience and spirituality – at which point he suggested that I present my position to the Multi-faith Group. Paul and I have a long-standing relationship so he knows my general position. This was a challenge and opportunity too good to miss!

As a result of many years of discussions, in particular with my friend Dr John Hey, formerly Head of Religious Studies at the University of Derby, and out of the thinking, reading and writing which I have undertaken, I have concluded that, at least at this time, I wish to call myself a 'nihilistic humanist'. In other words I believe in nothing and something. Some may see these two terms as rather self-contradictory. Others may think that I have not understood the concept of nihilism in its historical sets of meanings. However, the discussion which follows is an attempt to clarify what I mean and why I think that for me each of these terms is both necessary and descriptive of my position. A reference to an in-joke between John and myself: *I cannot see how to get off the treadmill of dualism.* It would not qualify as the world's most humorous one-liner!

I shall frequently use the term 'belief' throughout because, as my credo in the Preface indicates, I am a believer of sorts. I am a believer because I am presenting hopes, ideas, concepts, values which I cannot *know* to be correct or valid for any others but myself. They are not epistemological statements. It is in this sense that I am a 'believer' and hence I think that it is appropriate to be giving a lecture version of this book to the Multi-faith Group. When push comes to shove we are all, I suggest, in the believing (uncertain) mode and not the knowing (confident) mode.

Another introductory comment: I recognise that in using the term 'nihilistic' I am intentionally trying to shift away from any sense that my values are based on metaphysical or theological assumptions. Rather than deriving my values from metaphysical or theological presuppositions, I am constructing them against what I believe to be the meaninglessness of reality which is 'outside' human experience. That is the 'nothing' to which I refer. There is no meaning 'out there' to be 'discovered'. The universe has in itself no moral order. Meaning needs to be invented and it is people who do the inventing.

A lot of my discussion is devoted to saying why I believe in nothing. This is because it has taken me a long time to remove the layers of Christian and Enlightenment thinking which impacted on my meaning and thought. My being was embedded in them and infused by them. It is also because I had a confusing tendency to assume that 'belief' was 'knowledge', that is I tended to conflate fideism with epistemology. I thought that human knowing could access universal and certain knowledge. As D'Isanto puts it:

> Nietzsche speaks of 'nihilism' in order to give a name to the way in which nineteenth century philosophy experiences the impossibility of finding logical or epistemological access to universal foundational knowledge.   (1999: 1)

When I was a Christian believer, Christianity gave me notions of a universal purpose for life which originated with

God. This purpose included salvation from sin, a spiritual and moral basis for living, a belief in an essential 'me' which was my soul, and the notion of an eternal future in a perfected existence with other people/spirits and with God. The Enlightenment, in which I came to believe during and after I was ending my belief in God, gave me ideas of secular progress and the assumption that human knowledge would lead to truth and to human improvement. I now agree with Nietzsche's view.

I have tried to remove both of these sets of Christian and Enlightenment assumptions from my ways of understanding and beliefs and values, although it will be clear that in the case of my values, there are still residues of Judaeo-Christian valuing of people but not for theological reasons. I have needed to remove them because I have come to believe that the human species is the result of evolution, that I am therefore an animal, and that there is no such inherent, essential, universal 'thing' as human nature. That is why I say later that Darwin's ideas on evolution are the most important ideas that I have come across.

> Darwinism is a scientific theory that seeks to explain how things work, and to give an understanding of the origins of the world as we know it. But many ideas and problems about ourselves and our situation are of a kind that cannot be affected by scientific change, and others, which in principle may be so affected, are contingently unaffected by this one. Sorting out which ideas come into which category is a philosophical task, which is why philosophical analysis is essential for understanding the implications of Darwinism.
>
> (Richards 2000: 260)

I find that I have to believe, whatever my evolutionary origins, and as of now I believe in nothing and something.

The main sections of this book discuss the major aspects of my own belief system. I start with the necessity of believing and some of the problems which arise when believing transmutes into dogmatic and orthodox knowing.

I then discuss why I believe in 'nothing' and my approach to nihilism, in which I explore why I do not believe in any external (God derived) source of meaning.

Finally, I explore the 'something' in which I do believe, and in particular I state my values. These are basic to my sense of being and they are the source of my agency within the world.

On beliefs and orthodoxy

Of course, beliefs that are more likely to be accepted will survive and reproduce more than those that are not likely to be accepted! The question, of course, is what makes a belief more or less acceptable than another?   (Conte 2000: 88)

We must learn the art of conversation, from which truth emerges, not as in Socratic dialogues, by the refutation of falsehood but by a quite different process of letting our world be enlarged by the presence of others who think, act, and interpret reality in ways radically different from our own.   (Sacks 2002: 23)

'Is it true that mankind demands, and always will demand, miracle, mystery and authority?'
        (D.H. Lawrence, quoted by Gray 2002: 122)

I beseech you, in the bowels of Christ, think it possible that you might be mistaken.   (Cromwell 1650)

Beliefs are central to our human being. They are the building blocks of the narratives by which we create our sense of personal, cultural, social and, for some, religious identity. Beliefs are always present even when they are unconsciously held. These beliefs arise from histories which are national, local, religious and personal. They are instilled into us in childhood by stories, by role models, through the media and by inculcation. They are repetitiously reiterated in narratives, in myths, in cultural symbols, in norms, in the emphasised differences between 'us' and 'them' and in the meanings which we are (consciously and unconsciously) encouraged to give to our lives and to the lives of others.

Beliefs are not limited to the personal and social.

Beliefs inform our ways of being in the world. They essentially structure our understanding of the external world. They allow us to make our way through life without having to check out evidence for everything all the time – although in times of trauma and upheaval we may well find ourselves asking 'Why?', which is a cry for evidence of meaning and purpose. For much of the time we behave *as if* our beliefs were knowledge. We tend to confuse believing and knowing. We interpret our experiences through our beliefs about the assumed causes, sources and meanings of these experiences. Meanings of experiences are filtered through the beliefs which we have about our lives. Once instilled or adopted, beliefs are difficult to change because if we change our beliefs we also change our understanding of ourselves and of the world to which these beliefs apply.

Beliefs inform our public lives, our private lives and our fantasy lives. Beliefs create the world in which we live our daily lives.

Beliefs inform notions of where we came from, what to do now we are here and what will or may happen to us in the future and when we die. Beliefs not only inform but create our narratives of our past, our present and our hopes for the future. In brief jargon, beliefs construct our existential chronologies.

For some, their beliefs are couched in traditional religious creeds which are recited as part of religious rituals. 'I believe in God, the Father almighty, maker of heaven and earth' is the opening of one such Christian creed recited daily in many churches, and one of the creeds which are required, by law, to be repeated in Anglican cathedrals. This and other creeds locate the Christian believer's sense of self, of the *raison d'être* of the church community and of the origins and purpose of the world in the creative actions of a personal God. All religious creeds and texts have these origins/identity/community-creating functions. They are, among other things, sources of meaning.

For those who are not religious but who adopt a humanistic stance, their beliefs are not so easily encapsulated. They are not couched in well-known and oft rehearsed credal statements. There is no summary term such as 'God' which encapsulates a vast range of significant meaning. There are no humanistic buildings, such as churches, mosques or synagogues, in which the ritual of credal affirmations by religious communities are made. No hymns to be sung. Hence, for many such religionless people their beliefs seem to be both an individual matter and, for that very reason, a source of some confusion and a sense, perhaps, of isolation. There are humanist *associations* which hold meetings, but not what could be called humanist *communities*. Unless one goes to a church to repeat a credal statement of beliefs, there are few opportunities for either belief clarification or belief affirmation. And yet beliefs are nevertheless crucial to our sense of being and our engagement with the world. We cannot avoid them even though we may not be aware of them.

Joining a political party and voting at elections is one such opportunity. Going on demonstrations is a very visible statement of beliefs. The kind of work which we undertake is another. Some organisations now have 'Mission Statements' – with missionary intentions! The ways in which we socialise our children is yet another. The ways in which we manage and negotiate our relationships are also actions in which our beliefs are put to work, framed, affirmed, changed and challenged. Leisure activities, voluntary work, gifts to charity, our moral choices are all indicators of our beliefs. What we watch on TV and which newspapers we read are belief indicators.

But what these opportunities for the practice of humanistic beliefs lack is a community of believing and a community of action. Martin Jacques (2002) presented his views on the individualism of our society after spending three years in another, more communal culture. He expresses shock at how endemic individualism has become and how noticeable it was on his return.

Our beliefs are closely allied to our values and in turn these influence our actions, our sense of agency in the world. As I said earlier, our beliefs structure not only our self concepts but also our approach to the world and to our being in the world.

I will take three recent instances in which beliefs have come to have a very high profile. They arise from each of the world's major monotheistic religions: Islam, Christianity and Judaism.

The first example is quite literally world shattering. I think that 'world' is a metaphor. We often mean the shattering of 'meaning'. To experience shattering of meaning is a form of trauma (see Bracken 2002).

The horror of 11 September 2001 was created because of the belief system, values and actions of extreme and aggressive Islamic fundamentalists. The diaries and records of the suicide terrorists, subsequently discovered, indicate that they were obeying the will of the God in whom they believed. Their God – the one and only true God from their point of view – authorised the attempted destruction of iconic buildings of the evil empire known as America. Their God is one who, apparently, wills the destruction of people rather than either their conversion or conviction by persuasion. Certainly not a God who wills a plural society or a multi-faith world. The effects of beliefs and actions could not have a much higher profile in American and world thinking than this. Such extreme and dogmatic beliefs – not restricted to Islam – led a group of Muslim believers to the view that America is the epitome of international evil and alien values which should be destroyed. Thus a religious war against infidels – a jihad – is validated. Other beliefs of the suicide terrorists have been well rehearsed, including their belief that they would be going to paradise with attendant rewards and enjoyments. Their actions and martyrdom were justified, validated and even required by the God in whom they believed.

In 'The Suicide Bombers' (*The New York Review of Books*, 16 January 2003), Avishai Margalit includes the following:

> On a videocassette recorded before he was sent on his mission, he said: 'I want to avenge the blood of the Palestinians, especially the blood of the women, of the elderly, and of the children, and in particular the blood of the baby girl Iman Hejjo whose death shook me to the core … I devote my humble deed to the Islamic believers who admire the martyrs and who work for them …'
>
> From a religious point of view, a crucial element in being a shahid (martyr) is purity of motive (niy ya) doing God's will rather than acting out of self interest. Acting because of one's personal plight or to achieve glory are not pure motives. Most of the families of the shuhada (martyrs) accordingly want to present their suicides in the best possible light. To honour and admire the family of a shahid is a religious obligation and the family's status is thus elevated among religious and traditional Palestinians.
>
> (2003: 37)

I find the mixture of revenge and a sort of theological altruism interesting. God is clearly used as the ultimate authority to justify the killing of one's self, as valued martyr, and of others on whom God wishes to wreak vengeance. Thus the martyr's death and that of others are both willed and authorised by God.

Ruthven explores in great detail the background and context of this terror, and in particular notes:

> An essential feature of premillennial, apocalyptic fundamentalism that characterizes the Protestant tradition is its emphasis on personal salvation … The underlying morality is personal, almost narcissistic: I am a good 'saved' person. I struggle against evil not for the good of humanity, but for my own salvation … Apocalyptic thinking is also central to Islamic militancy, past and present. Given the cultural legitimacy or weight of authority conveyed by these

traditions, only a few small steps are needed for an actor to move from a 'religious' – that is, symbolic – understanding of the apocalypse to a historical one in which the divine imperative becomes an order to kill and be killed.

(2002: 34–35)

The underlying morality is narcissistic. A total lack of empathic awareness of the value of 'the other'.

I was present at a meeting at which a moderate, national leader of Muslims expounded his view that these extremists seeking martyrdom were not 'orthodox' Muslims. He did not have an easy ride from some of the young Muslims in the audience. But obedience to God is part of a religious believer's value system and guides her/his actions. Some Gods, and some versions of orthodoxy, appear to require stricter obedience than others. Some 'orthodox' Gods are evidently less tolerant of diversity than others – less moderate. Some Gods seem to be able to authorise the deaths of infidels because infidels are 'evil'. Some Gods seem rather narcissistic.

Diametrically opposed, but oddly similar, to this version of an Islamic fundamentalist belief system is the response of the American President George W. Bush. He too has decided to see the world in oppositional terms of 'good' and 'evil' – with the notable difference that those who are not *for* America are *against* America. In his case good and evil are thus inverted from the Islamic terrorists' concepts: 'God bless America'. In Bush's case the democratic freedoms for which America stands makes it the epitome of civilised values. The defence of these 'civilised values' allowed him to declare a war on terror. Thus another form of war is validated, not a war against a state or nation but a war against an idea. At first he declared a 'crusade' but was rapidly informed that this term had very unfortunate overtones in the Muslim world. 'Crusade' would come naturally to Bush because he is a Christian and a Methodist and therefore in the Protestant tradition. For him there is an 'axis of evil' which needs to be destroyed. Not human beings to be persuaded, cared for or converted, but destroyed. Iraq has been included in that axis of evil and was therefore subsequently included in that war – again in defence of American 'civilised' freedoms and with assertions as to the justification for 'pre-emptive attacks' – by America that is, not by others on America.

It's interesting that the pre-emptive attacks by the powerful against the weak are deemed to be valid, whereas the pre-emptive attacks by the weak against the powerful are invalid – indeed 'evil'. Bush has been warned by the leader of the Methodist Church in America that a pre-emptive war does not meet a crucial criterion for a 'just war'. But powerful people have strong tendencies to define others' realities for them, even legal realities. Powerful people define orthodoxies and orthodoxies, whether religious or nationalistic, do not brook challenge. Americans who have spoken out against the aggressive and imperialistic Bush approach have been castigated as anti-American – and in the name of freedom!

Believers who adopt strongly dogmatic versions of their beliefs tend to polarise the world into 'for us' and 'against us'. Good versus evil. I've come to think that dogmatic believing could be a symptom of a form of paranoia in response to a perception of threat.

Phillips proposes the notion of values as an escape: 'Values are born out of perceived threat' (2001: 55). Perhaps the threat is meaninglessness and the escape is escape from nihilism. Perhaps the threat is the danger of the invalidation of 'our' meanings, beliefs and values by those of 'the others'. 'We' risk being annihilated by 'them'. One of the attractions of religious belief is that an ultimate source of values and meaning is accepted, and a (comfortable and comforting?) community of believers is created. Comfortable if one belongs on the terms defined by the traditions and hierarchy of the community. The community also has its authenticating creeds – its self-affirmations. We are 'true' believers.

'Evil' may seem to justify going to war, but it could be seen as merely a validation of fear, of unreflective anger and the need for revenge. Rowan Williams (2002) explores this issue based on his experiences of being at a meeting within a few hundred yards of the twin towers when the attack took place. Labelling a whole country or a regime as 'evil' seems to create a sense that 'the other' is less than human. This then can be used to justify their extermination. This has been one reason for wars, pogroms and other such throughout history. Polarisation precludes any thoughtful discussion in the middle ground, although I am slightly relieved to think that the United Nations constitutes some form of 'middle ground'. A polarised debate is ended before it's begun. If the conclusion is prescribed, discussion is precluded. It is being increasingly said that the 'real' reason for the war against Iraq is oil. After all, the West backed Iraq against Iran some years ago when the interests of the West were different. Saddam Hussein's use of weapons of mass destruction against his own people then did not evoke the wrath, or even the concern, of the West. So much for the apparent simplicity of human motivation and of the espousal of 'civilised values' of freedom and democracy. 'Evil regimes' seem to be a moveable feast and seem to obfuscate real motivations and covert interests.

Who decides which regime needs changing? By whose authority, by whom and by what methods should the change be wrought? These questions beg issues of beliefs.

It does not take too much awareness of changes in the world since 9/11 to note that beliefs, in particular religious beliefs, have attained a much higher profile than perhaps they had before that day, particularly for those who have not consciously espoused any overt belief system. Books on Islam have suddenly leapt out on booksellers' displays and some have become best sellers. Many realised their profound ignorance of a belief system which had changed their (meaning) world and undermined their sense of security.

Beliefs do matter. They are central to our human being in

our relationships and in our approach to the world. As I said earlier, beliefs and related myths and imagery are the stories we tell ourselves about our origins, our identities. They represent our need for purpose and meaning. My meaning arises from needs to validate my existence and my human relatedness. A threat to my meaning is therefore in a sense a threat to my very existence. 9/11 was a threat to meaning as much as it was a threat to existence.

We await with trepidation the outcome of this clash of beliefs, values and meanings.

My next two examples are of lower profile (with respect to the two people whom I shall quote and the respective events) but each in its way points up some important aspects of beliefs – and the threat to, and from, others who believe differently. As with 9/11 they are examples of orthodoxy and dogmatism. They are brief case studies of current religious attitudes towards heresy. A friend smiled when I mentioned heresy. She thought that had disappeared in the Middle Ages. Sadly, not so.

Rowan Williams published *Lost Icons. Reflections on Cultural Bereavement* in 2000 when he was still Archbishop of Wales. I was particularly interested by the way in which his analysis of some current social and personal issues adopted what I took to be a very humanistic stance – he only mentions God three times in the first three chapters. He does not ostensibly make his social analysis of current problems depend upon an explicit elucidation of his Christian position, and certainly does not thrust his theology down the reader's throat. I enjoyed the book, agreed with a great deal of it and found it stimulating. I wrote to him to tell him so.

I then noticed in *The Guardian* (26 September 2002) that allegations of heresy were being made against him by two conservative Anglican evangelical groups, 'Reform' and the Church Society. They had called him to a meeting to explain his approach to the Christian scriptures and his positive attitude to homosexuality. They were also concerned that he had attended a pagan ceremony of the Welsh Eisteddfod at which he had been awarded an honour as a poet. It seems not to be an exaggeration to speculate that this issue may cause a theological split in the Anglican church. The *Guardian* report included the following:

> A meeting of the society's [the Church Society] governing council recently unanimously agreed to take a 'robust' approach to the new archbishop due to his reported heresy on issues such as the uniqueness of the Christian gospel. In an editorial this week, the reactionary *English Churchman* newspaper stated: 'it is not enough to tell [Dr Williams] that he should be silent about his views; it is not enough to tell him that he shouldn't rock the boat ... *he must be told he is in error* [my emphasis]. He must be told he is a false shepherd of his sheep; he must be told to repent his views'. David Phillips, the society's general secretary, said: 'Our fundamental concern is whether he is prepared to live by the teaching of scripture. I find his writings extremely difficult to penetrate. At the very least his views about sexuality are a matter of gross error. There are folk who wonder what is the point of staying in the church, and there are days when I feel that too'.

The Church Society and Reform are evidently in no doubt as to what is to be believed, who is to decide what is to be believed and of the source of that belief system. The two sources are the Christian scriptures and the Thirty-Nine Articles of the Anglican Church which define that church's beliefs. The fact that Williams is the new Archbishop of Canterbury and was Lady Margaret Professor of Divinity at Oxford count for nothing. The only thing which counts is whether he believes what the Church Society and Reform believe and assert that he should believe. And they (alone) know what true belief is. They have no problem with the crucial differences between 'belief' and 'knowledge'. For them, their beliefs are certain knowledge, and their knowledge leaves no leeway for doubt or divergence. This confidence is based in *their* belief that *their* knowledge is revealed by *their* version of God and on *their* interpretation of what they believe to be *their* scriptures.

In a report of the meeting with Rowan Williams on the *Sunday* programme (BBC Radio 4, 6 October 2002), their leader the Rev. George Curry said that they had come away 'deeply, deeply concerned because it looks as if we are to end up with an Archbishop who is prepared to endorse immorality and who is prepared to sit loose to the plain authority of the teaching of the Bible in an un-Anglican and un-Christian position'. The Church Society believes that they may have to repudiate Rowan Williams on his accession as Archbishop of Canterbury on the basis of the error of his beliefs. This may cause schism in the Church of England. The schism will be caused by those who assume that their beliefs are true and that their beliefs are firm and certain knowledge, not to be tampered with or undermined by a former professor of divinity who has become Archbishop of Canterbury and who, in that appointment, has received the backing of the forums of the Church of England. The beliefs of the Church Society are true – end of debate. God is indisputably on their side. They have the 'right' to decide on the content of revealed truth. There is no middle ground.

The similarity to the certainty of some Islamic fundamentalists is obvious. If you are not 'for' us you are 'against' us. Subsequently the Church Society in combination with Reform have called on Williams either to recant or stand down. 'The council … called upon loyal Anglicans to pray specifically that Rowan Williams would see the error of his teaching, change his views or stand down' (*The Guardian*, 8 October 2002). 'He is,' asserted the leader of the evangelical Reform group, 'undermining the authority of the word of God'. Not only is he un-Anglican, he is un-Christian. It seems not a trivial question to ask: how would God change the Archbishop's mind in response to prayers for him to recognise his error?

I find it interesting that the Church Society is different

from Reform. Even the orthodox find it difficult to tolerate each other. Although killing people who hold the wrong beliefs is still prevalent, the modest benefit is that they have merely attempted to assassinate his credibility and his authority to be Archbishop.

In the same week that I read Williams's book I had just finished reading Chief Rabbi Jonathan Sacks's book *The Dignity of Difference* (2002), which I also enjoyed. It takes the necessity for inter-faith conversation seriously. It assumes that no one faith has the whole truth about God. It argues the point that God has made people different and that therefore there is a divinely initiated dignity in difference. Difference is not reprehensible, but laudable. Difference is not something which should make us antagonistic to each other but which should create conversations which will be mutually enriching.

For saying this he too was accused of heresy (apikoras) by a group of rabbis who are orthodox Jews of which he is the Chief Rabbi. He too was called to a meeting to explain himself. This was included in the same *Guardian* report on Rowan Williams.

The next day (27 September 2002) *The Guardian* reported that Sacks had recanted and had agreed that a few changes to the offending sentences would be made in any further editions of his book. The rabbis were angry that Sacks had stated that no one religion had the whole truth about God and that conversation is necessary in order to expand our religious understandings. They, on the other hand, were asserting that their (orthodox) Jewish beliefs do indeed contain all the unique, complete and necessary truths about God. Sacks was urging that religions – which have traditionally been a major source of conflicts in the world – could become a major source of the solutions to conflicts if it was accepted that God had created differences and that these differences are to be viewed positively as sources of enrichment. This did not go down at all well with his co-orthodox rabbinical colleagues. Their orthodox Jewish faith has all the relevant truth about God and this truth does not need to be enhanced by any so-called truths from any other religions. Their orthodoxy is a complete and perfect revelation of God. The next day the Chief Rabbi's spokesperson stated that the changes to which Sacks had agreed did not alter the general thesis of his book. I disagree. I think that the fact that he agreed to changes at all undermined his tolerant thesis about the need for dialogue.

But things got worse for the Chief Rabbi. A subsequent report in *The Guardian* (18 October 2002) indicated a much more serious problem for him:

> The book, *The Dignity of Difference*, appears to be drawing increasing criticism because it suggests that all faiths might learn from each other.
>
> Orthodox rabbis have been outraged at the implication that Judaism may fall short of perfection. In an attempt at clarification yesterday Dr Sacks issued a statement insisting he had never suggested that Judaism did not contain absolute truth. But in an advertisement to be published in today's *Jewish Chronicle*, leaders of orthodox Jewish communities in London and Gateshead say: 'Any implication that Judaism does not contain absolute truth represents a grave deviation from the pathways of traditional and authentic Judaism' … the advert adds: '*We urge Rabbi Sacks upon reflection to repudiate the thesis of the book and to withdraw the book from circulation*' [my emphasis]. The passage which appears to have caused offence states: 'God has spoken to mankind in many languages, through Judaism to the Jews, Christianity to the Christians, Islam to the Muslims … no one creed has a monopoly of spiritual truth. In heaven there is truth, on earth there are truths. God is greater than any religion. He is only partially comprehended by any faith'. His critics claim it is part of a pattern during the 10 years of his chief rabbinate during which there have been rows about his attempts to propitiate the community over issues such as his participation in multi-faith gatherings like the Queen's Jubilee service at St Paul's last June.

He is said to be preparing a clarification, not retraction, to prevent further misunderstandings of his position. Not much dignity in difference then. Sacks stated:

> We must learn the art of conversation, from which truth emerges, not as in Socratic dialogues, by the refutation of falsehood but by a quite different process of letting our world be enlarged by the presence of others who think, act, and interpret reality in ways radically different from our own.   (2002: 23)

But the art of conversation is lost on his orthodox brethren.

A report in *The Observer* (27 October 2002) revealed that an orthodox Rabbi Elchonen Halpern has refused to call Sacks a rabbi and warned other rabbis that they must speak out against Sacks or lose their authority. Citing Proverbs 10.7 – 'the name of the wicked will rot' – he declared: 'He will not be forgiven for this sin until he makes proper atonement and recalls all copies of the book so that they may be completely destroyed as with all other heretical books. God forbid [that rabbis] should be suspected of their silence of agreeing with him and that there is some ambiguity'. There is a move from some ultra-orthodox factions to remove him from his position as Chief Rabbi.

So much for conversation. So much for listening and being heard. So much for the central thesis of Sacks's book for which I wrote to thank him. It seems that my gratitude might have been premature. And this is the twenty-first century and we are in the 'enlightened' West.

I began to develop a fantasy that any religious book of which I approved would quickly lead its author to face a charge of heresy! My approval seems like a kiss of death. My approval also seems to be something which these authors could well do without. It indicates, more seriously, that for religious people to write in ways which positively engage those who do not believe in their own faith position, even in the West and even in the twenty-first century, can be very risky. Those who adopt faith positions are sometimes dogmatic and they can become very defensive and anxious when their positions are challenged, particularly from 'within' as it were. It is clear to me that the beliefs of these two religious leaders are only valid in orthodox terms if they conform to others' notion of orthodoxy. Orthodox as defined by those who define themselves as orthodox by the criteria of scriptural texts and traditions which they have decided are the only valid texts and traditions and over which the orthodox have the only valid means of 'true' interpretation. Freedom of thought, or even variation of interpretation, is a basic threat to orthodoxy. Orthodox gods have apparently willed and revealed 'truth' – not debate and not conversation. The obvious fact that there are different orthodoxies with different 'truths' seems not to worry the orthodox of any particular faith – except to deny the validity of other orthodoxies. Perhaps an appropriate collective noun would be a 'confusion' of orthodoxies!

Dogmatic orthodoxy is very condemnatory of those who disagree or even differ. There is a clear belief demarcation between 'us' and 'them'. People who insist on their orthodoxy as being the correct belief system for others are exercising crude power and sometimes coercion over others' sense of being. Orthodoxy is oppressive. I can't help feeling that the more seriously people take their religious beliefs the less likely they are to be tolerant and the less likely they are to seek dialogue with others whose beliefs do not match with theirs.

Orthodoxy silences diversity. Orthodoxy does not listen – it talks. Orthodoxy is a monologue, not a dialogue. There is a deafness, and to me an inhumanity, about rigid orthodoxy. In fairness I need to say that not all religious systems are rigidly orthodox. Buddhism, for instance, values diversity and is not dogmatic. Dogmatism is the death of dialogue in that it perpetuates conflict rather than offering a dignified and co-operative resolution.

This is why I indicated above that Rabbi Jonathan Sacks's *The Dignity of Difference* is a moving and welcome commitment to belief in the benefits and the necessity of conversation (perhaps rather than conversion). He has a particularly interesting chapter, 'Exorcising Plato's Ghost', in which he criticises the Platonic/ Western notion of a universal truth which is believed not only to exist but which all should seek:

> My argument is far more fundamental, namely that universalism is an inadequate response to tribalism, and no less dangerous. It leads to the belief – superficially compelling but quite false – that there is only one truth about the essentials of the human condition, and it holds true for all peoples at all times. If I am right, you are wrong. If what I believe is the truth, then your belief, which differs from mine, must be an error from which you must be converted, cured and saved.   (2002: 50)

I strongly agree with his criticism of 'one truth' and I applaud his adoption of the validity of a plurality of beliefs. This, for me, is a genuinely strong sense of identity and subjectivity in which others can be allowed and even encouraged to hold different positions so that conversation is both possible and desirable for mutual enrichment.

His whole book is, for me, a surprisingly tolerant approach to the need for religious dialogue which eschews the certainties of dogma ('one truth'). In my letter to him I expressed, among other things, the hope that his conversation would include humanists who do not believe in any form of God and that his approach would dignify humanists as validly different. It's interesting to speculate whether a humanist has anything to bring to the enrichment of theological conversation.

Allied to the complexities of 9/11 these two case studies seem to give rise to fundamentally important and interesting issues about the origins and functions of beliefs, some of which are constructed into religious faith systems which may become aggressively fundamentalist. Such beliefs are likely to have one of the two following origins: the first religious, the second humanistic.

Religious origins

In the religious scenario, the commandments, scriptures, instructions, teachings, exhortations, goals for living, nature of society, requirement to worship, attitudes to non-believers and benefits/punishments included in religious beliefs are believed to be divinely inspired and divinely revealed. In this case they are likely not only to be accepted as *beliefs* but assumed to be *knowledge*. And not only knowledge, but immutable, unique and essentially true knowledge, true for all people and for all time. In this case the existence of definitive, revealed, usually ancient texts and traditions will be crucial. The interpretation of these will be in the keeping of suitably authorised people, in traditional religions usually men. There is also likely to be a hierarchy of priests/rabbis/imams who have a range of authority in relation to what is correct belief and behaviour for those who properly and fully belong to the group of believers. Rituals of induction and belonging will also be important – as will be the processes of exclusion. In extreme cases the attitudes to non-believers, infidels or heretics can include killing them, or at least 'inducing' them to believe or recant. I am reminded of the *fatwa* against Salman Rushdie and the politico-religious conflict in Northern Ireland.

In less extreme cases the true believers may engage in activities which are intended to lead to the conversion of the non-believers or the believers in the 'wrong' faith. These activities have led to global missions and imperialistic crusades. The previous Archbishop of Canterbury, George Carey, initiated an unfortunate 'Decade of Evangelism' some years ago. It did not thrive in a society which is multicultural and largely secular – or even indifferent.

Those who, like Williams and Sacks, argue for dialogue with non-believers and with believers in different faiths leave themselves open to charges of heresy. They are likely to be put under pressure to conform to the 'traditional' content of the belief system and to distance themselves from serious dialogue. Dialogue, in the form of conversation, means taking 'the other' seriously and therefore conversation is in some respects on the other's terms. Conversation is mutually respectful of other points of view. Genuine conversation is a commitment to change. Taking other people's faith and belief systems seriously is threatening to those who need to be convinced that theirs is the only and uniquely true belief/knowledge system. Sacks's heretical 'crime' is to be arguing that other faiths have aspects of truth which are worthy of attention in order to enhance the awareness of God's revelation in the Jewish faith – thus he was being accused of assuming that the Orthodox Jewish faith was in some respects lacking. This perception of 'lack' led to the accusation of heresy. In my letter to him I expressed the hope that his advocacy of conversation would include humanists such as myself. I doubt it, if even attendance at multi-faith services is banned by the orthodox of Judaism.

In the case of Williams, the conservative, evangelical 'orthodox' accused him of fundamental 'error' in relation to the scriptures and may refuse to accept his authority as archbishop. As I indicated, a schism is possible as one group of believers accuses another group of irredeemable error, and thus loss of proper authority. Valid authority depends, not on the fact of being human and being able to argue one's case, but on having the right beliefs as defined by the 'genuinely' orthodox.

The function of their beliefs, for these threatened and orthodox believers, is to assure themselves that they are 'right', that others are 'wrong' and that it is essential to protect and preserve the orthodoxy of being 'right'. This, even at the expense of putting enormous pressure on those who thought that they were within the orthodox rightness of the correct belief system – indeed who are national leaders of the respective belief systems. Pressure to believe and say the 'right' things has a most unfortunate history. The pressure is to conform, the goal is orthodoxy and control and coercion are the means to those ends. To be excluded is to be at risk.

What is the point of dialogue if you and you alone have

the truth? It must be a strangely comforting (yet defensive and aggressive) experience to believe that everyone in the world who does not agree with you is 'in error'.

Humanistic origins

The second scenario for a general origin of beliefs, this time from a humanistic approach, is the assumption that all beliefs are humanly constructed, are variable and are intrinsically open to critical and sceptical scrutiny. Such humanist beliefs therefore change over time because there is no way of providing ultimate validation and there is no source of traditional, revealed orthodoxy against which they have to be tested. Likewise, there are no official keepers of humanistic orthodoxy who require recalcitrants to toe the line. There is no heresy in humanism and there is no hierarchy in humanism. Neither is there an agreed credo. Debate is of the essence. It's a relief not be at risk of being accused of being 'in error'.

It needs to be said, however, that humanistic beliefs do not arise in a vacuum. They are embedded in cultures – and cultures include religious beliefs. As I shall be saying later, my own values and beliefs have arisen in a broadly Judaeo-Christian culture and have been influenced by what, in the West, has been called the Enlightenment. I did not make them up out of nothing; my culture gave me some building blocks. But I have given my beliefs a great deal of critical scrutiny over time.

As I shall also be arguing later, science is an important source of checking as to the validity of some forms of belief, and some beliefs change over time in response to scientific knowledge – few now believe that the earth is flat. Few believe that illness is a divine punishment for sin as asserted in the Anglican Book of Common Prayer. However, this human source and humanistic construction of beliefs does not depend entirely upon science as the source of validation. This is because science is incapable of answering all the kinds of questions which can be posed by people in relation to meanings, beliefs and values for life and living. Science can only deal with questions which are capable of empirical analysis and which are capable of being theorised in testable, evidenced and disprovable ways. I do not believe in *scientism* – the notion that only science is capable of providing all the answers to our questions. There are important distinctions between 'fact' and 'value'. Therefore I shall be emphasising that my position as a humanist is a belief position which cannot, ultimately, be proved or disproved by scientific analysis. My values and my belief in them are always uncertain, always open to debate, change over time and are not offered as anything like the typical sense of orthodoxy. This second source of humanistic beliefs is essentially uncertain. You may or may not find my beliefs and values persuasive. This could be seen as a 'weak' position, but it feels fine to me and, I think, is no 'weaker' than the ironical variety, and therefore uncertainty, of the range of so-called 'unique' orthodoxies on offer.

The first source of the content of religious beliefs is external to the human condition. The source in this case is divine. There is Someone external in whom to believe. This first is also, paradoxically, the focus of a wide range of different and equally certain orthodoxies, which suggests that it may be nearer the second than is presumed by the orthodox believers. Hence, for me, I was impressed by the cogency and humanity of Sacks's position on the dignity of difference with the exception that I do not believe in any form of God. Some of his colleagues were not so impressed.

The second source of beliefs and meanings is located within the human world and represents my position as a humanist.

One thing which I glean from these brief case studies is that religious orthodoxies seem to assume that they 'own' the God in whom they so strongly believe. In this way unorthodox 'others' are not allowed access to the 'owned' God except in terms defined and controlled by the 'owners'. The 'owners' are existential gatekeepers. Ownership and orthodoxy are essentially about power. There is a pernickety and pernicious pedantry about dogmatic orthodoxy. It worries me.

If there were only one truth, then those who had access to it would have only one thing, or only a few things, to say about it. Different religious orthodoxies assume that they each have access to the 'one' truth. A plurality of 'truth' orthodoxies of 'final' revelations is a contradiction in terms. It seems to be a fact that whether there is one truth or many, there are many things to be said because many things are actually said. From my point of view these 'many things' are all to the good.

As Cromwell urged: 'I beseech you, in the bowels of Christ, think it possible that you might be mistaken'.

My approach to nihilism

Nietzsche, in whom 'nihilism became conscious for the first time'. (Camus, quoted by Tarnas 1996: 411)

Viewed from a wide variety of perspectives one could rightly conclude that life itself is a pointless enterprise. That still would not preclude either its value or, for want of a better word, its beauty. (Spinelli 2001: 10)

We have entered an era of nihilism and within modernity there is no longer any stable structure to what is at stake for us. Power, as expressed in the calculative thought of our times, robs us of any coherent and generally accepted meaning for our lives. (Bracken 2002: 162)

To recognize the arrival of nihilism as a guest at our door – to use Nietzsche's expression – means to listen to the announcement of an event and to carry it to its logical conclusion. Vattimo observes that Nietzsche's thesis concerning the death of God is not intended as a metaphysical statement that might be demonstrated. On the contrary, it is the narration of an experience which is announced to others so that they too may discover the truth for themselves … Thus the announcement of nihilism has ethical and political implications. (D'Isanto 1999: 6)

I feel it is necessary to say at the outset of this section that it will take me some time to explain why I believe in nothing, that is, why I am arguing for a nihilistic position. This is because I have been inculcated with the results of centuries of the kind of thinking in which my own being, and that of being in general, has been located in a belief in a creator God. In this theological world-view there is no necessary problem about whether life has any meaning. It simply does, and the purpose of our lives is to discover God's meaning for our lives and then for us to live in accordance with this divinely ordained meaning. In this model the meaning of life is theological, and God's nature and demands are revealed knowledge accessed by faith.

I have also deeply assimilated assumptions which arose during and since the Enlightenment. In the Enlightenment approach there is a truth to be discovered, and then there is the necessity of living in accordance with this truth so that our lives can be validated by certain knowledge rather than invalidated by myths and stories. In this model the meaning of life is its being grounded in truth, and truth is epistemological not theological. This form of truth is accessed by discovery and by reason.

My approach to nihilism needs to be located in my broader philosophical thinking and in my strictly limited understanding of neo-Darwinian thought, current cosmology, quantum physics and neurobiology. For many years science has had a significant impact on my thinking about myself and the world. I have to assert 'strictly limited' understanding because, of course, if I waited until I had full understanding I would wait for ever and forever would be never. Maddox asserts that 'the scientific enterprise is an unfinished project and will remain so for the rest of time' (2002: ix). Ultimate truth is ultimately unachievable so therefore science cannot provide answers to questions of meaning and values. It is unlikely to provide final answers even to its own forms of questions in relation to the world. I conclude therefore that my beliefs and values, whilst informed by scientific knowledge, cannot be determined by that knowledge. I have the responsibility for deciding what values to live by.

A little knowledge is widely reported to be a dangerous thing, but a little knowledge is all I have to go on and all that I inevitably have to go on. Therefore my understanding will always be limited and of necessity I engage with the world on the basis of my beliefs about it because I can never know whether or not my beliefs are true. My 'strictly limited' scientific understanding is nevertheless important, not least because it allows me to develop some evidence for my beliefs about the world and my place in it. However, I am not able to transcend my beliefs about the world – or indeed my beliefs about myself – in a way which provides me with direct access either to the world or to myself. Nor do I believe this to be possible for others to do. In this I am obviously indebted to Kant and notions of the noumena and phenomena, that is 'things as they are in themselves' and 'our indirect perception of things in our awareness'. As Freud also said: 'Reality will always remain unknowable' (quoted in Nagel 1999: 15).

I cannot get outside my own beliefs to check whether they are ultimately true.

Somewhat more recently Gray put it as follows: 'To think of science as the search for truth is to renew a mystical faith, the faith of Plato and Augustine, that truth rules the world, that truth is divine' (2002: 20). I have neither a mystical faith in truth, nor do I believe that truth is divine.

I have to make sense of my limited understanding without access to the truth because, if I am to continue living, deciding and acting, I have to be an existential agent who lives 'as if' what I believe has some form of, albeit temporary, validity, not truth. My beliefs can be valid without being verifiable. I therefore agree with Davidson:

> Truth is not a value, so the 'pursuit of truth' is an empty enterprise unless it means only that it is often worthwhile to increase our confidence in our beliefs, by collecting further evidence or checking our calculations. (2000: 67)

I also sympathise with Trigg when he says:

> The crucial point about beliefs is not so much that they are ours. They must at least purport to be about something independent of the belief. Whether or not they are true is then a matter of what the world is like. (2002: 12)

However, in terms of beliefs about life and its meaning (lessness) I do not see how these beliefs can be ultimately tested by finding out 'what the world is like' because I suspect that total knowing what the world is like is not ultimately achievable. In any case, knowing what the world is like (empirically) is not the same as making meaning of what it is like. Lacking total knowing I have to make do with the 'little knowledge' which I have – dangerous or otherwise. Hence I believe things. Hence I *make* meaning – I do not *discover* it.

It is, of course, more than mere time for understanding which I lack. My fundamental problem is that I simply have no means of transcending the subject/object divide in order to arrive at direct access to things as they are in themselves. My knowledge is always mediated through what I already know and through my embodied mind which does the knowing. There is, I suspect, always a gap between what I think about reality by using the language with which I consciously think, and that *about which* I am thinking. There is, I suggest, no such thing as unmediated knowledge. Putting this succinctly:

> I think *about* things, I do not think them directly. My words are words *about* things, my words are not the things themselves. My thoughts and words about 'cat' are not the cat itself. The cat is essentially and always more than my thoughts and words about it. I cannot access 'catness' – or anything else – directly.

This is a simple statement to make but the implications are considerable. It means that there are insuperable barriers to the human mind having direct access to the outside world. Not only is it not possible for the human mind to have direct access to the world outside itself (everything comes to us through our senses), but there is a further problem. This is that the mind develops a range of symbols (language, mathematics, models) which are used to re-present the external world. There is no way of knowing whether these symbols actually, accurately and totally represent the things to which they are intended to apply. Science makes increasingly rigorous and successful attempts to bridge the gap between our knowing about the world and the symbols which are devised to encapsulate that knowing. Science makes impressive progress – and it works to a greater or lesser extent – but the problem of the gap between what we know and the thing which is to be known still remains. It remains insolubly.

And philosophy stumbles on the same problem. Hatfield puts this issue in the following way:

> Once we've given up the attractive view that the fundamental theory of the universe can be perceived through the *a priori* insights of the pure intellect, we no longer have a method by which philosophy can in one step move to the frontier of all human knowledge ... Because philosophers can't claim special non-empirical access to these core concepts or the structures of institutions we must engage with the world of experience – not merely by reflecting on our own experience but also by keeping up with knowledge and practice in any subject matter that bears on the objects of philosophizing ... To pursue Descartes' broad philosophical ambition we must replace the method of pure intuition with an immersion in, and engagement with, the achievements, uncertainties, and ongoing projects of our time. (2003: 331–32)

Direct access to reality is not available to the mind.

In his fascinating study of current research on the development of mind and thought in infancy, Hobson puts this philosophical point in a developmental context:

> In the first place, then, a person is aware of the distinction between having thoughts and perceiving things. In addition, and perhaps more obviously, the person is aware not only that thoughts are connected with things – after all, they are about things – but also that they are separate from and distinct from the things they are about. Thoughts are mental whereas things are physical. Thoughts and things have very different properties ... In other words, symbols do not really stand for things themselves ... Rather, the words

evoke particular ways of conceptualizing or remembering or experiencing the things. To be more precise, they evoke how the writer and the reader have experienced the things in question. Symbols ground ways of construing the world.

(2002: 96–97)

The symbols are our, frequently shared, ways of believing in the kind of world which the symbols symbolise. The symbols are essential to our ability to find our way around the world as we understand it. The symbols are the locations of our beliefs about the world. The symbols are the locus of the meanings which we create about the world. 'Symbols ground ways of construing the world.'

This leads to my view that there is an intrinsic dualism about my thinking. This dualism resides in the fact that I have symbols/beliefs about the world but that I am aware that these are never final and that the world may well be in some important respects other than that which I believe it to be. I believe in a form of monism such as that discussed by Papineau (2002) but I can never be sure that I have fully understood that single world. There are things, and there are my ways of thinking about things and there is my living in the world (see Farrell 1996 for a view of triangulation of world, culture and self). Thus I always have to live *as if* I know, but what I think I know is that I do not know. I believe – I have no choice, and therefore I am a believer of sorts. What I do have a choice about is the content of my believing. I am a humanist and therefore I believe that human beings create and invent the meanings by which they live. My beliefs are also subjected to critical scrutiny and therefore my beliefs about myself and the world are changing. My beliefs are valid for me even though they change over time. I am a sceptical believer. I would hate to be incarcerated in the prison of orthodoxy.

I suspect that if I had no sense of even a temporary validity of my beliefs then suicide would be a much more likely option than I feel it to be. I generally agree with Camus's position in 'The Myth of Sisyphus' that there is only one serious philosophical question and that is whether life is worth living. For him, all other questions are just details.

It's interesting, in passing, that the terrorist suicide martyrs seem so convinced of the ultimate significance and value of their own beliefs and their own lives, yet are so totally dismissive of the beliefs, values and the value of the lives of those whom they kill. There is a paradox here. Their God seems to will the destruction of his own creatures. This God's morality leaves a lot to be desired. The morality of narcissism as Ruthven (2002) observes. I find it very difficult to understand.

My basic nihilistic belief is that there is no meaning to life or for life which is external to the human embodied mind. There is, I believe, no theological or other form of metaphysical source of meanings, or of values, other than those sources which are human. There is, in my belief system, no teleological, no theological, predetermined or prepackaged goal or purpose to or for living other than those purposes and goals which human beings construct and to which human beings decide to commit. 'For the materialist, on the other hand, there is no question of finding out by looking at the universe how things ought to be, because the universe has in itself no moral order' (Richards 2000: 263). If the universe has no moral order then, I propose, it cannot be the source of meaning and values.

These human goals and commitments tend to be culturally specific, they vary for the individual over time and vary across and within cultures. They even vary within and across religions. Thus understanding the world is not a static Enlightenment, truth-attaining possibility. Vattimo (1999) even argues that there is a form of nihilism which derives from the failure of the Enlightenment project and I would agree with him. The failure is to establish a secure epistemological basis for knowledge.

I will risk a generalisation:

> As our understanding changes so in a sense the (our) world,
> changes. The limits of my understanding are the extent of
> my world – to misquote Wittgenstein.

My understanding, scientific and other, influences my beliefs. Science attempts, with considerable success in certain fields, to reduce this variability and discover universal aspects of what can be known and applied.

I do not believe that life is absurd, with some existentialists, because that would be to assume a value (absurdity) inherent in life. I do not describe myself as an atheist because that is a form of belief as negative theology. I believe life to be meaningless except for that meaning which I and others, communally and culturally, give it. There are, for me, no values and norms for living which transcend the human norms which are created by cultures and societies.

Some individuals develop an idiosyncratic view of the world which may become subsequently normative. For example, Darwin, Einstein and Freud had this effect, although in Freud's case this is more in the form of inventions and meanings than scientific discoveries. There is a sense in which we all develop forms of idiosyncrasy in meaning due to the uniqueness of our experiences. Our meanings are mixtures of the normal (shared) and the idiosyncratic.

My nihilistic humanism is not a dogmatic position, nor is the term 'orthodox' relevant. It is a fideistic position – it is believable for me. I have come to the view that all basic positions about life are fideistic in the sense that we cannot access anything directly but only create and invent our beliefs about them. 'The meaning of things lies not in things themselves, but in our attitudes to them' (Antoine de Saint-Exupéry, quoted on the cover of Grayling 2001). And, for my purposes, attitudes incorporate beliefs.

Critchley puts a view which is close to my own:

> Nihilism is the breakdown of the order of meaning, where all that was posited as a transcendent source of value in pre-Kantian metaphysics becomes null and void, where there are no cognitive skyhooks on which to hang a meaning for life. All transcendent claims for a meaning to life have

been reduced to mere values ... and those values have become, for Nietzsche, incredible, standing in need of 'transvaluation' or 'revaluation' ... For Nietzsche, nihilism as a psychological state is attained when it is realized that the categories [for Nietzsche the Christian-Moral categories] by means of which human beings have tried to give meaning to the universe are meaningless ... That is to say, nihilism is the consequence of moral valuation. My values no longer have a place in the world – it is this self-alienation of the modern Stoic that Hegel calls 'the moral view of the world' and which can lead to the resignation of nihilism, but which can also lead to a demand for a revaluation of values, the revolutionary philosophical demand that things be different. (1999: 11-12)

I tend to agree with Scott:

To live with no sense of ultimate meaning and with the sense that life's meanings arise as cultural images from no meaning at all and still want to live in affirmation of life opposes western understanding of affirmation. Life-giving hope, love, and justice have required an ultimate justification in most segments of our tradition ... And yet to learn at least the beginning steps of such affirmation suggested to Nietzsche a possibility for a kind of creature that is different from humans as we know them. (1999: 159)

In other words we have to take responsibility for the creation of meaning. We therefore also have the responsibility for deciding what to believe and on which values we want to act.

My nihilistic humanism shares fideism with religious positions except that they base themselves in belief in the existence of God who is deemed to take various forms in different traditions but who is the ultimate and external source of personal meaning and value and of existence itself. There are various ways in which this God seems to make himself (typically a male God) known: revelation by God of himself, special texts and credal encapsulations drawn up by 'special' iconic people, rituals, traditions, priestly hierarchies who transmit authentic beliefs, morality, assurances and forgiveness. Religious believers also tend to elide believing and knowing. Thus human meaning is dependent upon God's existence.

Not, however, for Nietzsche:

> 'Whither is God?' he cried: 'I will tell you. We have killed him – you and I. All of us are his murderers. But how did we do this? How could we drink up the sea? Who gave us a sponge to wipe away the entire horizon? What were we doing when we unchained this earth from its sun? Whither is it moving now? Whither are we moving? Away from all suns? Is there still any up or down? Are we not wandering as through an infinite nothing? Do we not feel the breath of empty space? Has it not become colder? Is not night continually closing in on us? Do we hear nothing as yet of the gravediggers who are burying God? Do we smell nothing as yet of the divine decomposition? Gods, too, decompose. God is dead, God remains dead. And we have killed him'.   (1974: 181)

When this God dies – as 'announced' by Nietzsche – or whose existence comes to be disbelieved, then human beings are left with the responsibility for their own meaning. There is no hiding place – but there is potential. Unlike religious orthodox believers, I am responsible for what I believe, but I am not accountable to any divine being for what I believe. My accountability is to my fellow human beings and to myself. As Schroeder asserts:

> God's death is welcomed because the world becomes something for humanity to create and by doing so it can recreate itself.   (1999: 623)

Taylor puts it:

> The unending play of surfaces discloses the ineradicable duplicity of knowledge, shiftiness of truth, and undecidability of value … God is death and death is absolute master.   (1987: 16 and 23)

Rather surprisingly Taylor is a theologian, although on reflection a number of non-theological people call themselves (a)theologians these days! I suggest that there are many more than mere theological implications which follow from the death of God. It seems to me that reliance on metanarratives (overarching belief systems) and any other external form of personal validation also 'die' with the death of God, and Taylor explores some of these.

My nihilism applies a form of Ockham's (1285–1347 CE) razor which I paraphrase: I try not to multiply entities beyond necessity. That is I try to believe in a minimum for which I think I have some, limited, evidence and I work from there.

So, in contrast to all these religiously believed sources of meaning I believe that my nihilism may well be the case, and it seems to me that there are forms and sources of evidence which provide a degree of validation of my position. Persuasive and suggestive that is, to me. None of the forms of evidence which follow intrinsically deny that the religious fideistic position may be the case but the evidence persuades me of the validity of my nihilism. Beliefs are not proofs, nor are beliefs truths, but my beliefs are related to the 'matter of what the world is like' (Trigg 2002) or might be like or is like in part.

It is, as I have indicated, important not to confuse belief statements with truth statements. Orthodox believers in many 'orthodoxies' do make this confusion. Fideology is not epistemology although the two may have important aspects of relatedness in terms of how we go about the business of creating knowledge and meaning on the basis of what we *believe* to be knowable and meaningful. I suspect that believing is more fundamental to our be-ing in the world than knowing. In other words, fideism precedes epistemology. Kornblith (2002) provides a discussion of aspects of the relationship between believing and knowing.

My nihilism is based, first, on my understanding of some current scientific thinking, and secondly, on my reflections on my own sense of subjectivity allied to a general pondering about life. I outline my sources of evidence for both arguments in the following sections.

I also indicate some of the meaning which I give to this evidence. Sometimes I feel about 'meaning' like Augustine felt about time – most people know what time is until they begin to think about it. John Barrow points up some of the puzzlements about time, one of which is: 'Does time have a future?' (2002: 30). As long as my life has a framework and sense of time passing which is fairly stable and comfortable then my life seems to have 'meaning'. However when that framework changes significantly – the death of a loved person, loss of job, retirement, divorce, illness, loss of God, serious loss of trust in a previously deeply trusted relationship, even periods of loss of sleep and so on – then meaning seems to become more tenuous and fragmented.

I notice also that meaning, like time, seems to become more elusive when I begin to think about it. Given that we, generally, seem to seek meaning, sometimes quite urgently, then perhaps any form and source of meaning is better than none. Hence I think that many people opt to believe in external sources of meaning because living without any external source of meaning is a lonely existential business. Fromm captured this anxiety in *The Fear of Freedom* (2001). But the supposed certainties, indubitability and authority of the external sources have costs and dangers. One cost is the requirement to be obedient to what others say we should believe. One danger is that those who are certain and who have power may develop an extreme hubris – a hubris which despises those of different certainties or those who have no certainty. To despise others may easily lead to a desire to destroy them and to their actual destruction.

> Indeed, perhaps a picture of knowledge without certainty will make us less ethnocentric and more open to other points of view and other ways of living. Jacob Bronowski, in the episode called 'Knowledge and Certainty' of his old television series 'The Ascent of Man' makes this point dramatically. Standing ankle deep in a concentration camp pool, he lets the ashes of millions of dead Jews sift through his fingers as he pleads with us to become less sure about

what we know. When it comes to knowledge, humility is the best policy. Certainty, indubitability, necessity, were all requirements for being more than human and always gave way before the clever skeptic … Skepticism, if you will, has become an essential ingredient of knowing rather than its arch enemy. Paradoxically, for Wittgenstein, knowing is at the same time not-knowing. One need not believe in what one knows; one can be, indeed is better off being, uncertain. (Genova 1995: 195–96)

I state my preference for the beneficial human potential of uncertainty and scepticism rather than the arrogance and danger (to others) of theological or ideological orthodox certainty.

Intimations of nihilism

Scientific influences

The final fear of biological explanations of the mind is that they strip our lives of meaning and purpose. If we are just machines that let our genes make copies of themselves, if our joys and satisfactions are just biochemical events that will someday splutter out for good, if life was not created for a higher purpose and directed towards a noble goal, then why go on living? Life as we treasure it would be a sham, a Potemkin village with only the façade of value and worth ... My goal is defensive: to refute the accusation that a materialistic view of the mind is inherently amoral and that religious conceptions are to be favored because they are inherently more humane.   (Pinker 2002: 186–87)

Since his [Descartes's] time, the method of seeking a priori insight into the real nature of things has been abandoned. Modern science now moves back and forth between theoretical conjecture and empirical evidence. The notion that the human mind has innate access to the fundamental properties of physics is no longer viable.

(Hatfield 2003: 322)

First, the scientific sources which at the same time inform and extend my understanding and yet leave me with a sense of puzzlement and nihilism. A sense of knowing and not knowing.

The following four points are intended to identify the reasons why I adopt my nihilistic position. I find them both suggestive and persuasive.

The likely age of the cosmos and its future

> Over the past few centuries, the earth has aged spectacularly.
> Its creation has been moved back from 6pm on Saturday
> October 22 4004 BC, as calculated by the seventeenth-
> century scholar and archbishop of Armagh, James Ussher, to
> a time and date some 4.5 billion years earlier. The story of life
> has been stretched back almost as far … To look forward we
> must turn from geology to cosmology. Currently cosmology
> suggests a future that, if not infinite, dwarfs the past as much
> as the depths of time that, we now accept, dwarf Ussher's
> exquisite estimates … Thoughts and memories would only
> survive … if downloaded into circuits and magnetic fields
> in clouds of electrons and positrons …   (Rees 2001)

I am not in a position to check these statements for myself
– and indeed this will be the case in all the evidence which I find
persuasive. However my acceptance of this concept of cosmic age
and of future time puts my own existence into a time frame which
has, for me, deeply existential implications. In brief, it reinforces
for me the insignificance of my personal sense of time. This
evokes in me an awesome sense of the brevity of life in general
and of my own few years in particular. This sense of brevity
creates in me a sense of existential vertigo. I can sympathise with
the Christian palaeontologist who, trying hard to maintain his
belief in God and the Genesis story, asserted that God had put the
fossils in place in order to mislead people into thinking that the
earth was very old. He too might have experienced a version of
existential vertigo.

I am not actually asserting that mere time-scale *per se*
necessarily demonstrates anything nihilistic in particular, but it
is one aspect of my sources which helps to persuade me that life
in general, human life in particular and my own life especially
do not have any external or cosmic meaning. Nor do I have any
sense or indication of teleological and personal purpose in the
imponderable aeons of time. Gould (1999) provides an interesting
discussion in his first chapter in which the Rev. Thomas Burnet

(1635–1715 CE) tried to grapple with emerging geological information and Christian revelation and faith. Gould's book is an entertaining exposition of ways in which Christianity had tried to retain its meaningful and theological validity in the face of the development of scientific knowledge. He also argues for the maintenance of Non-Overlapping Magisteria in which he sees a need for the separation of a magisterium of science covering the empirical realm, and a magisterium of religion which includes issues of values. The 'big bang' notion of how it all started seems vaguely reasonable to me. On this issue I am content to believe what scientists say, and I can change my beliefs accordingly. On the issue of values the 'big bang' is silent.

Darwinian and neo-Darwinian thinking

Notions of the development of life on this planet and of myself as an organism (animal) along with all the other organisms make it difficult for me to believe in any form of divine or metaphysical teleology or purposive plan. I recognise, of course, that for some it is possible to believe in such a teleology – even a personal and loving purpose – but this is no longer an option for me. It used to be, but it became intellectually unsustainable and emotionally redundant. The neo-Darwinian idea of the evolutionary process as 'replication with variation' is believable to me and it means, for me, an evolutionary randomness to the life process of which I am merely a contingent and random outcome. I do not have any emotional or intellectual difficulty with this. It seems to have the benefit of being supported by evidence and it makes some form of sense to me in my state of relative ignorance. If it is the case that the emergence of life was a random event, then my own life is a consequence of this randomness. I cannot see how randomness can be meaningful. (For a discussion of Darwinian issues see Rose and Rose 2000; Ruse 2002: 192.)

I agree with Daniel Dennett's assertion that Darwin's

theory of evolution is the single most important idea anyone has ever had:

> Did you ever hear of a universal acid? ... It is a liquid so corrosive that it will eat through anything ... Darwin's idea bearing an unmistakable likeness to universal acid: it eats through just about every traditional concept, and leaves in its wake a revolutionized world view, with most of the old landmarks still recogizable, but transformed in fundamental ways. Darwin's idea had been born in answer to questions in biology, but it threatened to leak out, offering answers – welcome or not – to questions in cosmology (going in one direction) and psychology (going in another direction) ... And if mindless evolution could account for the breathtakingly clever artefacts in the biosphere, how could the products of our own 'real' minds be exempt from evolutionary explanation? Darwin's idea thus also threatened to spread all the way up, dissolving the illusion of our own authorship, our own divine spark of creativity and understanding.   (Dennett 1995: 63)

More recently, Janet Radcliffe Richards (2000) has discussed the effects of Darwinian thought on a wide range of human issues such as ethics, responsibility, freedom and philosophical issues of knowing, showing that complex and possible implications of Darwinian ideas are still being worked out by those who take them seriously.

In Darwin's time his ideas of our origins were shocking. They threatened the very notion of humanity as the pinnacle of God's creation. They threatened the notion of our unique, divinely ordained significance. We were relegated to the animal league. The notion of ourselves as animals, and as the result of the mindless processes of evolution, is still threatening and indeed shocking to many. It challenges both our sense of origins and our sense of our own value. Certainly Creationists find the idea threatening but they are not alone.

In his discussion of the significance of Descartes's ideas Hatfield has this to say about evolution:

With the rise of Darwinian theory in the nineteenth century, the notion that organisms were directly created by intelligent design was rejected by modern science. This still leaves us with the problem of accounting for our perception that the parts of organisms serve different functions. Some philosophers suggest that evolution plays the role of designer, crafting the organism through the process of 'natural selection'. Evolutionary pressures 'select' successful structures, thereby building up design-worthy bodily structures. Others reject such explanations as mere metaphor. We are left with an open problem, resulting partly from the success of the mechanistic picture and partly from its incompleteness. (2003: 323)

Whatever the details of the 'design process' my belief in evolution results in my accepting that human beings are all equally the result of that process, and that we all belong to the whole of the living world from which we evolved. I am in that sense an offspring of all life. That, for me, is the 'open problem'.

The discovery of DNA

The evidence that the vast majority of discovered living creatures have the DNA structure in common, supports my belief in myself as simply an organism, albeit one whose biology happens to be able to develop a culturally created language within which and by which to be able to think about issues of the origin of species and the meaning of life, *inter alia*. The apparent fact that my own DNA only differs from that of other primates by about two per cent provides me with convincing evidence that I am an animal – albeit, I think, a thoughtful one (Gray 2002). Of course, the discovery of DNA supports Darwin's evolutionary theory and has added considerably to current developments of this theory. The rapidly expanding research in genetics is almost bound to have considerable effects on our views of what makes us what we are, our notions of responsibility for our actions and of the possibilities for human reproduction and choice of characteristics of children. Not to mention possibilities for longevity. Darwin's work not only challenged notions of divine origins of life, but also laid the foundation for the genetic revolution of which we are only at the beginning.

Jeremy Rifkin's article 'Dazzled by science' (*The Guardian*, 14 January 2003) indicates some of the experiments and outcomes of the merely recent aspects of the genetic revolution:

> Already in laboratories around the world researchers are creating new hybrid creatures that have never before existed. Scientists have fused together the embryos of a sheep and a goat, two totally unrelated species, and given birth to a new creature called a Geep, a chimeric animal with the head of a sheep and the body of a goat ... Human growth hormone genes, the human immune system and even human brain tissue have been inserted into the genetic blueprint of mice embryos. The mature mice express these human genes in their bodies. The mice with the human growth hormone grew twice as big as ordinary mice. Scientists have even grown human skin, pancreases and breasts in laboratory jars. Other scientists have inserted the nucleus of a human cell into a cow egg whose own nucleus was removed in a partially successful attempt to create a quasi-human embryo ... Japanese scientists have just announced that they are planning to use tissue from the legs and testicles of a dead mammoth to clone the extinct creature and 'display' it in an Ice Age wildlife park in Siberia ... Life, long thought of as God's handiwork, and more recently viewed as a random process guided by the 'invisible hand' of natural selection, is now reimagined as an artistic medium ... the biotech revolution is the ultimate consumer playground, offering us the freedom to recast our own biological endowment and the rest of nature to suit whatever whim might move us.

These scientific, and to some people blasphemously bizarre and inappropriate, experiments are indicative of the genetic revolution. Like the industrial revolution before it, this revolution enables us to exercise control but it also forces us to consider who and what we are. It even gives us the possibility of asking and answering questions about who and what we want to be.

Quantum physics

My understanding of quantum physics is at a similarly superficial level to my understanding of cosmology, DNA, genetics and the processes of evolution. Even so, what I hear and read about it adds to my nihilistic position. I note that at the quantum level there may be parallel universes. String theory attempts to link 'weak' and 'strong' forces with gravity to produce a 'Theory of Everything'. Smolin provides a reasonably accessible discussion of quantum gravity (2001). Quanta can seemingly produce an effect prior to the cause but with total uncertainty as in Schrödinger's cat. Black holes make nonsense of notions of time and space as we know them with our perceptual apparatus. Then there is black matter and black energy.

This was the conclusion of the Melvyn Bragg *In Our Time* programme (BBC Radio 4, 10 January 2002) in a discussion with physicists:

> *John Gribbin:* We describe ourselves as carbon-based life forms. The carbon that's in all of us was created originally in the heart of a star. That is a powerful concept and something which we only became aware of in the twentieth century with nuclear physics.
>
> *Bragg:* So this is where we can get back to the idea of origins?
>
> *John Gribbin:* This is very much my own pet interest: the relationship between ourselves, humankind and the universe at large. We are products of the stars, we are absolutely literally stardust.
>
> *Bragg:* I can't think of anything to say after that … I feel quite exhausted …

I too find it difficult to follow both intellectually and existentially, but stardust I am – or so I am prepared to believe. I am stardust which became biological and I am biology which developed a particular form of brain, and my brain allows consciousness and I am consciousness which developed language and with that language I have developed ways of thinking about myself as stardust.

And in this sense I believe myself to be part of the everything which is, in that my existence depends upon what is (I am a version of a materialist monist), but not in a cosmic 'mind' or 'soul' sense.

These notions may not even disturb the religious believer (see my reference to Polkinghorne on p. 112 below) but they leave me not only perplexed – they actually exacerbate my sense of random contingency. They persuade me that: 'there is no question of finding out by looking at the universe how things ought to be, because the universe has in itself no moral order' (Richards 2000: 263). Fact and value are different. Facts are discovered. We decide on values.

An important point which I take from all this is that things are not as they seem. The 'reality' within which I live is based on the biologically based perceptual apparatus which I have and the cultural constructs which structure my perceptions and my language. Changes to my biological perceptual apparatus and to my cultural constructs would necessarily change my 'reality'. In future we may be able to see more than the 'visible' spectrum (by means of implants or virtual vision?) and the world would look different. However, I do have a degree of trust that my perceptions of reality represent that reality in more or less reliable ways. I do not believe that reality is totally the creation of my mind. There is a reality and the human mind has ability to understand it at least partially, and particularly effectively when operating in a scientific and rational mode (Nagel 1997; Sokal and Bricmont 1998). However, Hatfield's cautionary observation is relevant: 'But the notion that the human mind has innate access to the fundamental properties of physics is no longer viable' (2003: 322).

It will be evident that the impact of scientific discoveries on my way of thinking and on my beliefs has not caused me to transfer my belief in God to belief in science *per se*. My understanding of science has had two opposite and related effects: it has extended and informed my knowledge about the world in which I live; and it has acted like the eroding universal acid in Dennett's analogy.

In particular the idea of evolution has profoundly influenced my notions of who and what I am. I recall first coming up against evolutionary theory when I went to college aged 18. At the time I was an evangelical Christian so I had a few problems with evolution. As I indicated earlier, I am now convinced (prepared to believe) that I am an animal which is able to use language. Thus evolutionary thinking has had a profound effect on my sense of meaning. The understanding which I glean about the age of the universe and its possible future has also profoundly influenced my sense of brevity and hence the meaning which I can give to that brevity. Quantum physics throws my normal (Newtonian) sense of the daily world into a spin. It profoundly challenges my sense of causality and of stability. Science has both enhanced and enriched my understanding and contributed to the removal of my beliefs in a metaphysical source of meaning for life.

Tarnas puts this simultaneous expansion and contraction tension rather well:

As the twentieth century advanced, modern consciousness found itself caught up in an intensely contradictory process of simultaneous expansion and contraction. Extraordinary intellectual and psychological sophistication was accompanied by a debilitating sense of anomie and malaise. An unprecedented broadening of horizons and exposure to the experiences of others coincided with a private alienation

of no less extreme proportions. A stupendous quantity
of information had become available about all aspects of
life – the contemporary world, the historical past, other
cultures, other forms of life, the subatomic world, the
macrocosm, the human mind and the psyche – yet there was
also less ordering vision, less coherence and comprehension,
less certainty ... The anguish and alienation of twentieth-
century life were brought to full articulation as the existen-
tialist addressed the most fundamental, naked concerns of
human existence – suffering and death, loneliness and dread,
guilt, conflict, spiritual emptiness and ontological insecurity,
the void of absolute values and universal contexts, the sense
of cosmic absurdity, the frailty of human reason, the tragic
impasse of the human condition. Man was condemned to
be free. He faced the necessity of choice and thus knew the
continual burden of error. He lived in constant ignorance
of his future, thrown into a finite existence bounded at
each end by nothingness. The infinity of human aspiration
was defeated before the finitude of human possibility. Man
possessed no determining essence: only his existence was
given, an existence engulfed by mortality, risk, fear, ennui,
contradiction, uncertainty. No transcendental Absolute
guaranteed the fulfillment of human life or history. There
was no external design or providential purpose. Things
existed simply because they existed, not for some 'higher'
or 'deeper' reason. God was dead, and the universe blind to
human concerns, devoid of meaning or purpose. Man was
abandoned, on his own. All was contingent. To be authentic
one had to admit, and choose freely to encounter, the
stark reality of life's meaninglessness. Struggle alone gave
meaning.   (1996: 388–89)

This extract lucidly captures the paradox of the expansion of
understanding and the drastic reduction of coherence, meaning
and confidence. It almost seems as if, following the 'death' of
God, human experience fractures and fragments. This in turn
helps one to realise how seductive belief in God is for many
people, even in a diluted 'power greater than ourselves' form.

Belief in God could be construed as the avoidance of existential incoherence, fragmentation and meaninglessness. Belief in God could be seen as an escape into ready-made meaning. But it is also the avoidance of the acceptance of responsibility for creating one's own sense of meaning.

Science is the most powerful tool which humans have created for asking the kind of questions which can be answered by the use of carefully constructed and changing hypotheses, theories and methodologies – answers which can be falsified. Harriet Swain (2002) provides a fascinating sequence of leading scientists' brief responses to questions with which they are engaged: if ever you are tempted to think that all the main questions in science have been answered then this is the book to disturb your complacency! The results of scientific question-posing and empirical research provide answers, or potential answers, about those aspects of the world which can be observed (either directly or via technology) and about which theories can be constructed. Not, I hasten to add, answers which are true for all time, but answers which are relevant to the kinds of questions which were posed. Science proceeds on the basis of evidence, but evidence is always challenged and sometimes the evidence is misunderstood and misinterpreted. Nevertheless, this evidence can have a profound effect on what scientists and other people come to believe about the world and of possible meanings of their place in it. Cetina (1999) and Longino (2002) explore complex social, cultural and political ideas and values which frame scientific questions and the technology on which these questions depend for answers.

I have already provided examples of some ways in which scientific knowledge has affected my view of the world and of myself. It is, I think, reasonable to conclude that the application of rationality and other forms of careful thought in response to features of the world actually works. Science can reduce some aspects of uncertainty and produce useful technology which works – although quantum physics seems to undermine even this certainty. Scientific knowledge also needs to be treated with scepticism and the results and application kept under democratic control. These values of scepticism and democracy, too, are an application of values to the outcomes of science. These values are not inherent in science, they are 'value added'.

It is the belief that such a scientific approach can be validly extended to all aspects of life which I am resisting.

However, some scientists seem to have replaced God as the ultimate source of truth and meaning with science itself as the ultimate source of knowledge and therefore of meaning and value. Wilson is one such. *Consilience: the unity of knowledge* is a fascinating discussion of his *belief* that science can and will enable us to know everything:

> Preferring a search for objective reality over revelation is another way of satisfying religious hunger. It is an endeavor almost as old as civilization and intertwined with traditional religion, but it follows a very different course – a stoic's creed, an acquired taste, a guidebook to adventure plotted through rough terrain. It aims to save the spirit, not by surrender but by liberation of the human mind. Its central tenet, as Einstein knew, is the unification of knowledge.
>
> *When we have unified enough certain knowledge, we will understand who we are and why we are here* [my emphasis].
>
> (1998: 5)

> We have begun to probe the foundations of human nature, revealing what people intrinsically most need, and why. We are entering a new era of existentialism, not the old absurdist existentialism of Kierkegaard and Sartre, giving complete autonomy to the individual, but the concept that only unified learning, universally shared, makes accurate foresight and wise choice possible.   (1998: 332)

You will note that Wilson is actually expressing a belief which goes way beyond the evidence. He too, it might surprise him to know, is a believer. Not only that, his belief is metaphysical and therefore beyond scientific testing. I think that his belief is profoundly and misleadingly optimistic. It is misleading because Wilson seems to assume that the discovery of knowledge (science) is the same as the invention and construction of meaning. He is assuming that the unification of scientific knowledge will necessarily result in 'accurate foresight and wise choice'. Scientific knowledge is not necessarily liberation for the human mind. He is nothing if not an optimist. It is surely worth pausing to note that scientific knowledge and its effects – both actual and potential – on the environment may, for the first time during the period of the existence of life on this planet, destroy significant swathes of life on the planet by the actions of a form of life on this planet – human beings, sometimes known as *homo sapiens.*

To put this succinctly: scientific knowledge does not result either in wisdom or in improved self-management. This is because science does not directly produce knowledge of values. Rather, scientific knowledge is the object of decision-making by the application of human values. On values in science see, for example, Longino (2002: 51–52).

I have tried to make it clear that my limited understanding of scientific knowledge does have an impact on the meaning which I try to create for my life, but that meaning is more than the sum of the scientific knowledge which I have accumulated. Science is but one factor in the meaning which I invent. My meaning includes my values, and these are not necessarily related to scientific knowledge.

I suggest that Wilson's belief statement is also misleading because I suspect that we could never know whether we have understood everything – including the mind which is doing the knowing. In other words, I think that Wilson, along with many religious believers, is confusing 'believing' with 'knowing'. He is making a profoundly metaphysical statement. Only if there was a stable, knowable reality and a stable mind which is totally distinct from that stable reality could there be a chance of the human mind understanding everything. Which is a rather complex way of saying that our minds cannot understand everything because they are part of the everything which they are seeking to understand. In an even more succinct form: we are embodied minds. There is no epistemological way of verifying the foundations of our knowing. Hence we are left with our beliefs and our modes of believing.

Pinker offers what could be construed as a slightly more limited, and I think more realistic, view of the role of science:

> 'Man will become better when you show him what he is like', wrote Chekhov, and so the new sciences of the human mind can help lead the way to a realistic, biologically informed humanism. They expose the psychological unity of our species beneath the superficial differences of physical appearances and parochial culture.   (2002: xi)

I am persuaded by this notion of 'biologically informed humanism', and I think that it is important in that it captures both the evolutionary aspect of our species and the human areas of culture and choice. He quotes a lengthy and interesting list of 'human universals' compiled by Donald E. Brown (435–39) in support of the view that there are biologically determined/influenced human characteristics which contribute to the underlay of human nature.

Nagel seems to leave even more options for human reason and open thought:

> Try as we may, there is nowhere to escape from the pretensions of human reason. If we try to reinterpret it in a more modest fashion, we find ourselves, in carrying out the project, inevitably condemned to forming beliefs of some kind or other about the world and our place in it, and that can be done only by engaging in untrammeled thought.
>   (1997: 99)

'… engaging in untrammeled thought' is not naïve acceptance of confusion, but positive recognition of complexity and of the potential for the formation of reasonable – and changeable – beliefs and values out of this complexity.

It is important to emphasise that science cannot respond with evidence (knowledge) to all the kinds of questions which human beings pose about themselves, about meaning, about morality, about purposes of living, about our emotions and about beliefs and values for living. Meaning, morality, purposes, emotions and beliefs and values are not susceptible to scientifically evidenced answers (see Heath 2002b in which I criticise scientism's tendency to totalitarianism). When posing questions about meaning, morality, purpose, emotions and beliefs and values, it is evident that the 'answers' vary across cultures, within cultures, across religions, within religions, and even within the same person over time. I include emotions in this crucial list for two reasons: emotions infuse our reactions to all events and experiences no matter how rational our responses, and emotions provide value-laden aspects of our reactions to relationships, to our sense of reality and to our very consciousness (see Damasio 1999).

It is also obvious that people make meanings for their lives even when they have no knowledge at all of science. Meaning for life cannot depend on scientific knowledge although scientific knowledge may well influence the meanings which some people, in a scientific culture, create. I agree with the biologist Steven Rose that:

> Life is about both being and becoming; we are in a state of constant transformation ... within constrained necessities comes the freedom to choose, to act, and to build towards not only our own future but that of the whole of humanity and the planetary economies in which we are embedded.
>
> (2002: 230)

Even if the optimistic belief entertained by Wilson did become possible, there would then be the problem of convincing all the other non-scientists that science had found the 'meaning' of life, the universe and everything. That would be some educational task. It would be the ultimate problem identified by Bacon: knowledge is power. Science would then have become the ultimate orthodoxy. There would be no room for dispute. Science would indeed have replaced God. The 'dignity of diversity' of Sacks's book would have been ended – and he might once again find himself accused of heresy!

I conclude that there are no 'true' answers to meaning, morality, purpose, emotions and beliefs and values. There are many answers which are validly different. As I said above, my acceptance of neo-Darwinian notions of evolution leads me to the belief that I am an animal – albeit an animal which is capable of asking questions as to meaning. But my acceptance of what I believe to be convincing scientific evidence that I am a result of evolution does not in any certain respect provide an answer to my questions as to the meaning of my life. It does however, for me, rule out a whole raft of divinely dependent meanings which I used to adopt and which many others still adopt. Creationists think very differently about Darwin's work and subsequent developments. But the result for me is that I have to grapple with issues of my meaning as a product of evolution. It is a struggle to identify ways in which I can give meaning to my life. As I shall state later, my values are an essential aspect of my meaning. They are not scientifically verifiable, nor are they scientifically falsifiable, in fact they are not scientific at all – but they nevertheless seem to be reasonable and valid to me. I have a degree of confidence in my values, but not the kind of confidence which is associated with the results of scientific enquiry nor the (over) asserted confidence of the religiously orthodox.

My values enable me to make the following kinds of decisions and actions with confidence and with a sense of valuing my own and others' existence. My values give me a sense of confident agency in the complicated human world.

> Should I make a donation to the organisation which supports victims of torture? Certainly. I have no doubt about it. There is clear benefit.

> Should I agree to stem cell research and therapeutic cloning? Certainly. I have no doubt about it. The benefit is clear to me.

Should I desist from killing those people who make me angry or who hold beliefs which differ from mine? Certainly. I have no doubt about it. Others benefit from my valuing of them!

Should I oppose war against defenceless civilians? Certainly. I have no doubt about it. They may not actually benefit from my values because others may decide to kill them.

Should I reciprocate trust in my friendships? Certainly. I have no doubt about it. Again, I believe the benefit to be clear and mutual.

Should I spend time puzzling about my beliefs and values? Certainly. It seems to me to be a very valid activity because it is an important way in which I create my sense of meaning and by which I try to validate my life.

All these, and many more, confident responses derive precisely from my value system. My values allow me to engage with the world and with people in particular kinds of ways. So, I have no doubts about some aspects of my values and how to apply them in my daily living. But this is not scientific certainty. It is a consequence of my believing in certain values. And these values are not the kinds of things which science can 'observe' and empirically analyse. It is also the case that my values might change, but not easily.

Two further things also need to be said: There are complex situations in which I am not at all certain as to how to apply my values, or even if my present values are relevant. I do not always apply my values even though I know what actions my values require – I act hypocritically.

My values are an essential aspect of my subjectivity. They establish what I believe in and how I try to live.

> Once we enter the world for our temporary stay in it, there is no alternative but to try to decide what to believe and how to live, and the only way to do that is by trying to decide what is the case and what is right. (Nagel 1997: 143)

My sense of subjectivity

There are even times when 'merely to live', as Seneca put it in a letter to Lucilius, 'is itself an act of courage'.
(Grayling 2001: 21)

In the four centuries of modern man's existence, Bacon and Descartes have become Kafka and Beckett.
(Tarnas 1996: 394)

Among the imaginary constructions created by the intellect working in the service of the will, perhaps the most delusive is the view it gives to ourselves – as continuing, unified individuals. (Gray 2002: 44)

The second main source of my nihilism arises from my reflections on my subjectivity and pondering life generally, all of which lead me to a nihilistic position. To repeat: my nihilism is based on my belief that I have no epistemologically validateable access to the source of being. I have no access to any source of meaning outside human being. I am stuck with: '… the impossibility of finding a logical or epistemological access to universal, foundational knowledge' (D'Isanto 1999: 1).

Orthodoxy and identity

My own sense of subjectivity has changed over time and has included a range of beliefs. At one time I was an evangelical Christian and 'knew' that I was a child of God. There have been times when I did not know what to believe. At such times I also lacked a strong sense of who I was. It seems to me that there is an existential relationship between beliefs and identity.

The sheer multiplicity of human belief/meaning systems suggests to me, not that meaning is an *a priori* – that meaning exists outside or prior to belief systems. Rather that human beings who have developed forms of language and are therefore able to pose questions, seem not only to have a need to create knowledge, but also to believe that their created knowledge means something 'beyond' the fact that they created it. The search for knowledge seems to me to be at the same time a search for meaning. And the search for meaning is the search to validate my subjectivity. My meaning creates me. People are *knowledge discoverers* but *meaning makers*. Inventors, not the discoverers, of meaning. And there is a myriad of meaning and belief inventions. Some people do not seem to bother with attempting to check the veracity of their belief inventions – they merely believe them with intensity and 'belief' metamorphoses into 'truth' and this 'truth' all too often becomes orthodoxy. And this can happen in science as well as in religion and in politics, indeed in any dogmatic ideology which meets needs for strongly believed meaning.

Intense believing is related to a need to establish one's sense of subjectivity. Dogmatic orthodox believing is therefore an assertion that one's subjectivity is 'normal' and acceptable. But such orthodoxy is the death of development. To believe in an impermeable, dogmatic orthodoxy is to assume that what I believe is the only valid truth in which to believe. This form of orthodoxy only changes by permission of the orthodox. Orthodoxy is a 'truth' and therefore a form of power. Orthodoxy is living with existential blinkers. Orthodoxy is therefore the imprisoning of subjectivity. Orthodoxy is a form of obedience to others' imposed beliefs. For such people fideism becomes epistemology – belief becomes knowledge. And knowledge becomes 'certainty' as to who I am. For the religious believer, her/his being is on the right side of truth. I think that dogmatic believing indicates a fragile sense of identity.

Orthodox truth purports to correspond to reality.

I strongly agree with Davidson that it is useful to attempt some reality checks and that 'truth' is an idea which can be profoundly misleading:

> Truth as correspondence with reality may be an idea we
> are better off without … truths do not come with a 'mark',

like the date in the corner of some photographs, which
distinguishes them from falsehoods. The best we can do
is test, experiment, compare, and keep an open mind. But
no matter how long and well we and coming generations
keep at it, we and they will be left with fallible beliefs. We
know many things, and will learn more; what we will never
know for certain is which of the things we believe are true.
Since it is neither visible as a target, nor recognizable when
achieved, there is no point in calling truth a goal. Truth is
not a value, so the 'pursuit of truth' is an empty enterprise
unless it means only that it is often worthwhile to increase
our confidence in our beliefs, by collecting further evidence
or checking our calculations.   (2000: 66–67)

For the orthodox their beliefs have 'the mark' of truth on them.

There are complex relationships between knowledge and
existential issues. My beliefs are integral to my identity and sense
of subjectivity.

Changing identity

I now have no sense in my own experience either that God exists
or that I experience anything which I might reasonably call God.
Of course there is plenty of evidence that others do believe in God
– as indeed I used to myself – but I am not persuaded by numbers
of believers, nor by the status of some of those who believe nor by
the longevity of theological beliefs. I also do not think of myself
as being an 'infidel' by changing from being a believer in God to
being a believer in myself. I sensed at the time that my change
worried other people more than it worried me. But I did not find
it easy, nor was it quick. My religious phase made me less tolerant
and more restricted in my general awareness. It also made me
very defensive. I consciously resisted various kinds of threatening
knowledge. I was also wary of people who clearly and verbally
differed from my beliefs.

  These radical changes in the way in which I understood

myself seem to me to be developmental and enhancing. They expand my conscious sense of self and of others. I actually feel more human – although I recognise that that is a strange thing to say.

> A religious solution gives us a borrowed centrality through the concern of a supreme being. Perhaps the religious answer amounts to antihumanism, since we cannot compensate for the lack of cosmic meaning with a meaning derived from our own perspective … Some of us feel a constant undertow of absurdity in the projects and ambitions that give our lives their forward drive. These jarring displacements of the external view are inseparable from the full development of consciousness.　　　　　　　(Nagel 1986: 210–11)

I like his phrase '*a borrowed centrality*'. It is true for me that losing my belief in God and finding a form of (confused) belief in myself actually assisted the development of my sense of self and of consciousness of myself. Changing my beliefs changed my sense of identity.

Reasons and causes

In my own sense of subjectivity I do not find any awareness of reasons for why things happen to me other than by my own decisions, by those of others and the general randomness of living. There do not seem to me to be any God-like explanations or reasons or causes for events. I do not understand the causes of the vast majority of events, but that ignorance does not lead me to posit a divine cause. Belief in God does not appear to me as a valid solution to my ignorance. Whilst my ignorance is not bliss, attributing reasons to the existence of God would not be bliss either. I try to find reasons, but often have to settle for not knowing. I can live with uncertainty. I do not know the causes of most events in my life.

> While we should expect that good things will happen to bad people, and vice versa, we should not expect that there will

be a theoretically interesting answer to why things happen
that way. There will only be particular answers that relate to
the emergent effects of the actions taken by many people in a
finite world of which they have finite knowledge. Moreover,
because of the number and kind of factors invoked, these
answers will not say anything especially revealing about the
validity of any specific normative orientation of the world.

(Fuller 2001: 192)

I agree with Fuller when he questions any sense of the 'normative
orientation' of the world. I also agree with the idea that there can
be 'no theoretically interesting answer as to why things happen
that way' – or indeed as to why things happen any way. This
neatly says what I believe when I say that there is no meaning in
the world *per se,* there is no normative value, reason or purpose to
be discovered. There are meanings to be made, or meanings to be
constructed in terms of actions and events, in terms of the past,
present and future. 'To put this in the most general philosophical
terms, the disenchantment of theodicy amounts to the removal
of teleology from accounts of nature' (Fuller 2001: 194).

There is, I believe, no disembodied, culture-free purpose,
reason, cause, meaning or direction. Similarly, and in passing, I
do not believe in disembodied people. That is, I do not believe
in ghosts.

Free will – a mind field

This notion of 'normative value' impinges on another big issue
of human be-ing: that of free will. If there is a 'normative value'
(God) to which our own wills need to be attuned in order to
achieve some form of predetermined goal and purpose, then
what becomes of 'free' will? Free will, in so far as I understand this
vague notion, seems to require that I am free to make my own
mind up without being accused of reneging on some pre-existent
spiritual or religious/divine norm or a 'right' way to live. Free
will also seems to require that our will/mind acts independently

of the causal relationships which we normally assume to be operative. It is therefore deeply dualist in the Cartesian sense of dualism. In Cartesian dualism there is the mind and then there is everything else and the mind can act upon the 'everything else' in ways which affect both the mind and the everything else.

Nagel has this to say about free will:

> I change my mind about the problem of free will every time I think about it, and therefore I cannot offer any view with even moderate confidence; but my present opinion is that nothing that might be a solution has yet been described. This is not the case where there are several possible candidate solutions and we don't know which is correct. It is a case where nothing believable has (to my knowledge) been proposed by anyone in the extensive public discussion of the subject. (1986: 112)

I too have difficulties with the notion of free will. If there is a God who has devised a normative, value-laden world then I do not see how notions of autonomy can validly include the rejection of belief in God without fundamentally violating one's own (God-created) normative being. So, in the religious meaning framework, the unbeliever is 'normatively deficient' or is living in existential deficit. On the other hand if there is no God, as I believe to be the case, then the exercise of free will has no intrinsic moral value, but is only relevant in a cultural context in which particular notions of mind, responsibility and accountability to other people obtain. At this time, my notion of free will is that I have some degree of choice about which values to adopt and I have some limited choice in how to live by these values. I have no easy answer to the issue of what appears to be free will. It is, for me, a philosophical and psychological minefield. When I include the current, contentious, debate about the potential, albeit complex, influence of genes on behaviour and even personality traits and proclivities I become bogged down. I still believe that I have some (?) version of freedom to choose but I fail to satisfy myself in this belief. As with other aspects of my beliefs and values, I live as if it were so. Most of our social and political systems, as well as personal relationships, depend on the assumption of this metanarrative of the individual who is free to choose – the legal system is but one example. Dennett (2003) propounds the view that freedom evolves with the increasing ability to think symbolically and with increased levels of language skill. He makes serious attempts to provide an approach to free will which I find convincing:

> Free will is real, but it is not a pre-existing feature of our existence, like the law of gravity. It is also not what tradition declares it to be: a God-like power to exempt oneself from the causal fabric of the physical world. It is an evolved creation of human activity and beliefs, and is just as real as such other human creations as music and money.(2003: 13)

The slippery self

I have yet another perspective which seems to me to militate against the idea of external sources of accessible meaning. This is the very issue of my subjectivity: my sense of being a self who is conscious and aware.

My subjectivity, and consciousness of my subjectivity, has a number of aspects which I seem unable to deny – or at least not able to deny easily, and none of which seem to me to lead to an external source of meaning or epistemological validity. My basic sense of self – my subjectivity – seems to be a combination of aloneness and relatedness, choice and constraint, awareness and ignorance. There are many issues around this statement, one of which is related to consciousness, but I shall not pursue these here except to observe that notions of 'self' and 'individual' are not universal in cultures but are especially strong in Western thought. The following indicate aspects of my subjectivity which seem important enough for me to mention.

There is my sense of subjectivity which is at its most isolated and intense as when I am in severe pain, or fear or in high ecstasy or indeed when I am concentrating hard on the matter in hand. The world itself can almost fade away and I am overtaken by emotion or concentration. The world is present to me but only in a most restricted sense and in a way in which my own needs are paramount.

There is my sense of subjectivity when I am critically reflecting on the billions of years of the cosmos, on the sheer randomness of *that* sperm fertilising *that* egg instead of any other of 50,000,000 sperms, and on my mortality. I could have been anybody else. I may never have been at all. When I am gone I shall not be, in the same way that I would not have been had I not been born. There is a 'not being' or a potential for not being at the heart of my existence and I cannot will that 'not being' away. That 'not being' is also emphasised by what I believe to be the fact of my subjective end – the end of consciousness – and of my mortality. This particular sense of subjectivity gives me my deepest sense of existential vertigo. I have occasionally 'lost' my hold on my sense of being and of any meaningful reality. Not pleasant but a consequence of the belief system with which I choose to live.

> The individual person, like the species of which she is a member, is going nowhere discernible (or predictable), and nowhere in particular. But this is not so much a cause of grief as an invitation to go on inventing the future. Once our death doesn't matter to anyone else but us – not to God, or gods, or nature itself – it matters in a different way. Once there is nothing (or no one) overseeing it, it begins to look different. Darwin and Freud invent new deaths for us.
>
> (Phillips 1999: 29)

The notion of the invention of 'new deaths' is a typical Phillips turn of phrase.

There is my sense of subjectivity when I am conscious of being in third person mode. That is, when I am looking at someone, some situation, some thing. I am on the outside of the situation or the other person or the object trying to look in. From my point of view, this third person mode is still an aspect of my subjectivity. I cannot stand outside my subjectivity even in third person mode. I cannot take 'The View from Nowhere' (Nagel 1986). It seems that I spend most of my time in this third person mode of subjectivity. I spend a lot of time 'looking out' at other people and the world. Oddly, I also seem to be able to look at myself (looking in), which is what I am doing in this book. These 'looking out' and 'looking in' modes can seduce me into thinking (believing) that I am observing the world as it is. I can even be seduced into believing that I am actually observing myself. But on reflection, the world and myself are not necessarily as they appear to me. I do not have direct access to the world or to other people. I live with phenomenal inferences. My thinking about the world is a way of believing. I think *about* and talk *about* the world and myself but what I think and say is not necessarily verifiably true. My believing is fallible. I can tell you what I believe, but I cannot tell you that what I believe is true. The origins of my beliefs are not entirely clear to me. 'We cannot believe as we please; our beliefs are traces left by our unchosen lives ... As with other animals, some lives are happy, others wretched. None has a meaning that lies beyond itself' (Gray 2002: 18 and 48).

There are also difficulties with the notion of what is true:

> There may be many uses for the word 'true'. But the only one which could not be eliminated from our linguistic practice with relative ease is the cautionary use. That is the use we make of the word when we contrast justification with truth and say that *a belief may be justified but not true* (my emphasis) ... We pragmatists, who think that beliefs are habits of action rather than attempts to correspond to reality, see the cautionary use of the word 'true' as flagging up a special sort of danger. We use it to remind ourselves that people in different circumstances – people facing future audiences – may not be able to justify the belief which we

have triumphantly justified to all the audiences we have
encountered.   (Rorty 2000: 4)

Further quotations from Nagel and from Freud are also relevant:

> The question therefore arises in what sense is it possible to
> think about a physical system in mentalistic terms, taken
> from the vocabulary of experience, perception, desire, and
> the like, without having any idea of the physical significance
> of these descriptions ...   (Nagel 1999: 14)

What might the relationships be between our vocabulary and
that to which our vocabulary is applied? There are numerous
answers to this question, none of which is definitive.

And Nagel quoting Freud:

> In our science as in others the problem is the same: behind
> the attributes (qualities) of the object under examination
> which are presented directly to our perception, we have to
> discover something else which is more independent of the
> particular receptive capacity of our sense organs and which
> approximates more closely to what may be supposed to be
> the real state of affairs. We have no hope of being able to
> reach the latter itself, since it is evident that everything new
> that we have inferred must nevertheless be translated back
> into the language of our perceptions, from which it is simply
> impossible to free ourselves ... reality will always remain
> unknowable ... we infer a number of processes which are in
> themselves 'unknowable' and interpolate them in those that
> are conscious to us.   (Nagel 1999: 15)

'*Reality will always remain unknowable*'. We frequently translate
our perceptions into language. They are always mediated through
our embodied senses. There is not space to pick up this issue
here, but I repeat it because of its significance for me. Suffice it to
say that if reality will always remain unknowable, then my sense
of self is always bound to be slippery because it cannot be based
on certain knowledge.

> Meaning is bound to discourse; there is no meaning outside
> the symbolic space of culture.　　　　　　(Ferrari 2002:7)

There is my sense of subjectivity when I am aware of my location
in the limitations and possibilities of the culture and language
which enabled me to develop a particular sense of self, an 'I' and
an identity. This includes myself as a cultural artefact. I cannot
imagine what I would be without the culture which made me.
This is a sort of critically reflexive subjectivity – I puzzle about
the nature of my subjectivity. Once again the terms 'I', 'self',
'mind', 'identity' are very slippery and much contested in the
literature and research as well as being a problem when subjected
to introspection. Like 'time' and 'meaning' subjectivity seems to
elude careful scrutiny. I am left with my culturally constructed
beliefs about these key terms. I suspect that I cannot know the
'mind' as it is, nor the 'I' as it might be … *reality will always
remain unknowable.*

Being a self is a slippery experience. Some people (persistent
vegetative states, drugs, brain lesions) lose their sense of self (see
Ramachandran and Blakeslee 1999).

The slipperiness of self is one of the themes addressed
by Rowan Williams in *Lost Icons*. In this book he is critical of
the notion of a static, essential self and I agree with his general
approach to the narratival flexibility of self which I see as a
surprisingly humanistic approach to the self. I say 'surprisingly'
because he does not explicitly base his discussion on theological
premises but on some contemporary secular writings:

> Every 'telling' of myself is a retelling, and the act of telling
> changes what can be told next time, because it is, precisely,
> an act, with consequences, like other acts, in the world and
> speech of others. The self lives and moves in, only in, acts of
> telling – the time taken to set out and articulate a memory,
> the time that is a kind of representation (always partial,
> always skewed) of the time my material and mental life has
> taken, the time that has brought me here. To step aside from

this kind of telling and retelling, this always shifting and
growing representation of the past, is in effect to abandon
thinking itself or language itself ... the already experienced
knowledge that I am 'irretrievably dispersed in a multiplicity
of unstable feelings and changing relationships' in the words
of a recent and formidably original interpreter of Hegel,
Walter Davis.   (2000: 144–45)

My sense of self, and indeed my sense of others and of the
world, all these change even as I think about them. Not only
do I create different narratives or 'tellings' of myself over time,
but these narratives take on different meanings when I begin
to be aware of them and to think about them in relation to the
narratives of others and the world. My subjectivity is anything
but static and therefore my world is anything but static. Just as I
think that I am unable to understand 'the mind' as it is, so I am
unable to understand my 'mind'. My 'mind' and my 'self' and my
'identity' are all slippery in the same way – they do not exist as
objects of thought.

> ... the mind is inherently embodied, reason is shaped by
> the body, and since most thought is unconscious, the mind
> cannot be known simply by self-reflection.
>
> (Lakoff and Johnson 1999: 5)

I dealt with some of these issues in my article 'Philosophy and
Psychotherapy: Conflict or Co-operation?' (Heath 2002a). The
impenetrability and unknowability of the unconscious should
not be forgotten.

My sense of self is intrinsically linked to the restricted area
of awareness experienced by me as my consciousness. I have no
direct access to my consciousness nor to my unconsciousness.
My thinking about consciousness is available to me in narratives
and my narratives are social in origin and social in meaning.

> Consciousness as an 'account of ourselves' therefore proves
> necessary because we are animals who partly construct our
> accounts of ourselves because we are accountable 'as selves'
> to others, and this exchange of accountability again has a

> spiral instituting character ... Narratives which emerge at the layer of surface behaviour are particularly important, for all performance is understood within the context of the social group. At a fundamental level narratives are performed as rituals and myths, both of which have the instituting effect of maintaining a corporate memory. Myths supply a framework of images, in narrative form, in which the needs, values and fears of a group – in short, an articulation of emotions within a network of social consciousness – can be expressed.   (Clocksin 1998: 115)

Cornwell's *Consciousness and Human Identity* (1998), in which Clocksin's essay appears, is a fascinating collation of current thinking and research on this basic topic.

My sense of subjectivity changes. My sense of identity changes over time and in different contexts and in response to different understandings. I notice changes even in response to changing moods (in the short term) and certainly in response to changing my beliefs and values in the longer term. Thus at one period in my life my sense of subjectivity included, indeed derived from, my sense of dependence on God. This is not the case now and this is a considerable change in my shift from heteronomy (dependence on God) to relational and interdependent autonomy. Autonomy always needs to be carefully qualified by and located in interdependence. It's interesting to reflect on how and why personal changes in self and meaning take place.

There is my sense of subjectivity when I am in a close relationship in which I feel understood, affirmed, appreciated, valued. The closeness is not a fusion, but it is a sense of relational empathy. It is rather rare but the more welcome for that. Such relational empathy does not transcend my subjectivity but is a form of it.

There is the 'problem' of my subjectivity when I am asleep or under anaesthetic. Dreams, with their sense of reality, are also part of my subjectivity. LaBerge says: '... dreams are much more accurately described as experiences – that is conscious events that one has personally encountered' (2002: 61). He quotes Havelock: 'Dreams are real while they last. Can we say more of life?' (62). I was amused by the Havelock quotation. I cannot handle these issues in any clear way, but some of them are discussed from a neurobiological point of view by Greenfield (2000). Papineau (2002) explores issues of consciousness from a philosophical perspective.

A deeply ingrained aspect of my subjectivity is my scepticism. I seem to have always been sceptical even when I did not give voice to it and even when I believed in God. I think, on reflection, that my scepticism has stood me in good stead, and continues to do so, but it has not made for an easy existence.

An awareness which seems to me to permeate these aspects of my subjectivity is that they all depend necessarily on my body being the mediation between my self and the world. I do not, nor can I have, direct access to the world, to others, or even to my self. I say this last because even my access to my self is mediated by the cultural forms of language within which I have been constructed. My sense of being a self at all is totally dependent on the body which enables the embodied mind to exist (Varela, Thompson and Rosch 1996; Lakoff and Johnson 1999; Humphrey 2002). The words which I use about myself are not a private language (Wittgenstein argues against the idea of a private language and I agree with him) but the very words are embedded in cultural metanarratives from which I sense that there is no escape. Having said that, I also agree with Lyotard's injunction to adopt an attitude of 'incredulity towards metanarratives' (Lyotard 1979: xxiv). I notice that even though I adopt such incredulity I seem to inhabit, unavoidably, a metanarratival existence. It is within my metanarrative of nihilism and my beliefs and values and ways of knowing that I create my narratives of being-in-the-world.

These reflections about the nature of my subjectivity all contribute to my statement that I believe in nothing. It does not mean that I believe that there is nothing at all except my own existence – I am not a solipsist. It means that I do not believe in any meaning or any foundations of my subjectivity existing *a priori*. I have no sense that my subjectivity depends upon God's existence as the creator of either the world or of my subjectivity. I also have no sense of my subjectivity being reincarnated.

The sense which nihilism makes for me is a denial of theological, metaphysical, teleological notions of purpose. It is also a denial of the dependence of the self on the Self of God. 'The death of the sovereign God now appears to be the birth of the sovereign self' (Taylor 1987: 25). It seems important to me that I try to be clear about what I am not. This clears the ground for me to try to think about what I believe I am.

The fact that I value living and value myself and value others means that I need values for living. I shall develop these values below. I live my life *as if* I and others have value, but only a value which 'we' determine. 'We' is not a universal 'we'. I do not believe that there is a homogeneous value system. I do however, following Pinker and Richards, believe that there are universal tendencies for human beings to create values.

As I said at the beginning of this section, it has, somewhat ironically, taken me a long time to say that I believe in nothing. That is, in part, because there is a complicated 'I' who is doing the believing in nothing. In part it is because it is complicated to try to remove the layers of religious and metaphysical overlay which has created layers of thought within which I have been socialised. It has taken me a long time to become aware of this overlay and to consider my own position in relation to it. Working out alternatives to deep cultural norms is not easy.

In summary, I do not believe that there is any meaning to my existence other than meanings which I and we manage to give to our existence. 'The meaning of things lies not in things themselves, but in our attitudes to them' (Antoine de Saint-Exupéry, quoted on the cover of Grayling 2001).

Again to my pleasant surprise, I agree with the new Archbishop of Canterbury who elegantly summarises:

> I can only be where I 'truly' am by recognising that there is no fixed place where I am innocently and timelessly alone and incorrupt. And the recognition of how I 'negotiate' is what gives me the material for a telling of myself … a self is only really definable in the act of self-questioning, reflecting on the self can't be a way of thinking about an 'item' that will stay in focus while we look at it. The act of questioning is the act in which the self is itself. (R. Williams 2000: 146)

It is through my own process of questioning and reflecting that I have come to a view of myself and my values which provide me with a some sense of coherence, satisfaction and bases for action – but also deep and unresolvable uncertainty. This paradox is pointed up by Williams: *the act of questioning is the act in which the self is itself.*

It is the recognition that there is nothing about meaning and values there to be discovered in the world, but that meaning and value are creative inventions of human beings in their search for relational and other forms of meaning that could be seen as the essence of nihilism, or at least of my nihilism.

It is actually a positive position which allows values to be taken with more seriousness than the mere assumption that they exist in the world by metaphysical or theological fiat and that human life is about conforming to that which exists independently of it. The 'more seriousness' is the freedom that human beings have of the possibility of choosing their values in ways which are potentially for their benefit. That which can be chosen can also be changed. Such freedom is clearly related to notions of autonomy rather than heteronomy. Responsibility, choice and change are the seriousness to which I refer.

This approach in some respects is similar to the line taken by Wittgenstein in *Philosophical Investigations* (1953). In stating that 'philosophy is therapy' Wittgenstein is asserting that the belief in metaphysics as the source for the validation of human knowledge produces essentialist and universalist thinking which limits, and perhaps even undermines, the philosophical as well as the human project. The denial of metaphysics is emancipatory in the sense that it asserts that there are no metaphysical causes and/or sources which have to be discovered and lived by. There are choices and inventions for human beings to live by.

There are, I assert and believe, no sources of meaning outside myself (for example God or other forms of metaphysics) to discover by faith, revelation or reason which would validate meaning for me or for others. I accept, of course, that some others believe differently. Science is based on discovery. Human living is based on the invention of meanings. The 'fact' and 'value' distinction again.

There are sources which are in a sense 'outside' me (the world, other people, scientific knowledge, aesthetics, literature and so on) which I can use in order to create my own sense of meaning. I do not mean 'create' in the sense of total independence, but in the sense of creative interdependence. These sources are also 'inside' me by processes of assimilation and by my socially constructed language. Just as I think that my sense of self is relational, so I think that my sense of meaning is relational. Thus meaning is a personal, cultural and social artefact rather than an external given to be discovered. Meaning is constructed and conveyed in narratives, infused by other symbols and emotions. Hobson (2002) explores the origins of thought, self, identity, a sense of the objective existence of others, the development of attitudes to people and objects from observational studies of babies. He contrasts normal developmental processes with those of children who are autistic. His arguments and the supporting research confirm my own views that a sense of self – even the ability to think – is relational and not an inherent given.

As I live both in the day-to-day and in the existential context of my sense of past, present and future, I find that I have to act in the world. I have to make decisions, I have to relate to others. To be a non-agent does not seem to be feasible, unless I decide to commit suicide or, if in unrelievable pain and anguish, decide to seek for assistance in this matter. Of course suicide itself is an act of an agent in relation to the self and the world. In the case of religiously motivated suicide (martyrdom) it is a profoundly value-laden act with a view to effecting post-suicide changes in the world for other people (the destruction and demise of evil capitalism to take but a recent example). It is also value-laden with respect to the anticipated benefits which are believed to accrue to the person who commits suicide – paradise with virgins waiting, or whatever version of (male) gendered afterlife is believed in.

In the case of a nonreligious or nihilistic suicide, it could be construed as a statement that the person has not found a value-based reason for living. Purposeful and existentially sustainable meaning has not been created, and therefore the most valued act is the act which ends the valuelessness of living. Suicide could also be construed as an act of aggression towards others and/or an act of aggression towards oneself. In a sense such a form of suicide is a statement of a value – the value that life without meaning or a life of such depression and despair is not worth living.

In all these cases I sense that there are values around either implicitly or explicitly. However, not objective values:

> Nothing has any objective value, because objectively nothing matters at all. If we push the claims of objective detachment to their logical conclusion, and survey the world from a standpoint completely detached from all interests, we discover that there is nothing – no values left of any kind: things can be said to matter at all only to individuals within the world. The result is objective nihilism. (Nagel 1986: 146)

Nagel doesn't actually agree with this point but I find it interesting all the same.

As I indicated earlier, meaning is rather elusive when one begins to think about it. Whilst my life has a framework and I feel generally comfortable within that familiar framework, then life seems to have 'meaning'. However, when that framework changes for whatever reason then meaning seems to become more tenuous and fragmented. Meaning for life is so peculiarly difficult to pin down that I suspect that 'any' meaning is better than none. This is why I think that people have strong tendencies to believe in religious and other forms of spiritualisms or ideologies – because living without some apparently external form of meaning is very difficult to cope with. A current belief system, in which I have had involvement and about which I have written (Heath 2000; 2002a) is that of counselling and psychotherapy which, given the intensity with which it is believed, appears to offer, for some, a replacement for religion.

On this issue of a need to believe, I've been listening to Arthur Miller reading extracts from his book *The Crucible in History*. He refers to the 'poetry' of the witch-hunt in Salem in 1692:

> Poetry may seem an odd word for a witch-hunt but I saw now that there was something of the marvellous in the spectacle of a whole village if not of an entire province, whose imagination was literally captured by a vision of something that wasn't there.

There were no witches in fact, but the fact is that there were witch-hunts and many were burnt.

He is likening the witch-hunts of Salem to the intense paranoia of American society during the anti-Communist purges of the 1950s. It could be happening again in the notion of 'an axis of evil'. We not only have a proclivity to believe, but to believe in that which does not objectively exist so that we can pit ourselves against it and seek to destroy it. In this case, the believer's sense of being needs an opposition to affirm the believer's being. What we believe seems somehow less important than that we believe something which validates our lives by dependence upon that which seems to be more than, greater than, our lives. People seem to develop strong beliefs which have no evidential base for them because of a need for meaning. And the need for meaning can be elicited both by what we are for and what we are against. Hence the prevalence of 'good' and 'evil'. Living with the opposition of these polarised 'realities' provides a sense of being valid. It seems that we can know who and where we are when we polarise the world. I suggest that people who need to live in a highly polarised world of 'us' (good) and 'them' (evil) are doing so in order to establish and maintain a strong, but perhaps fragile, sense of personal identity. 'Strong' only in the respect that they do not need to consider the complication of grey areas of doubt, uncertainty or the recognition that others may have a valid point of view. Polarised meaning is defensive meaning, and defensive meaning defends identity.

Dogmatic orthodoxy could be seen in this light – as a highly defensive strategy to ensure a strong sense of identity and to avoid the recognition of other people's diverse validity. Orthodoxy avoids complexity. Perhaps this is why Sacks's book *The Dignity of Difference* evoked such strong anxiety among his orthodox colleagues. The anxiety is that their sense of identity is being undermined by his assertion of the validity of other religions.

Orthodoxy, religious or otherwise, is a means of defending a threatened identity.

Beliefs and meanings seem to be in a reciprocal relationship. I think that it is important to explore the 'what' and 'why' of belief not least because of the impact of my believing on others and my attitude to those who I call my fellow human beings. I try to construct my own values in ways that avoid a strong sense of excluding others. I try to live without the comforting benefit of polarisation. I try to value the inclusivity of diversity and difference.

Valuing difference and diversity leads me on to my beliefs and values. These constitute the 'something' in which I believe.

Believing in something

My approach to humanistic beliefs and values

Humanity's sense of beauty, and decency, our power to love, our creativity – all the best things about us – belong to us, to human experience in the real world. They neither need, nor benefit from, some alleged connection with supernatural agencies of one kind or another. They are ours, just as much as the evil, stupidity, greed and cruelty which they oppose.

(Grayling 2001: 124)

We do not know what we are doing but we have things that we must do.   (Phillips 2002: 13)

Thus, philosophers who attempted to ground ethics and science in the ultimate judgements of an all knowing being were mistaken. We can live rationally without having to believe in a being who sees everything. We need only believe in the ethical principle that observers should communicate honestly what they see. If we stick to this, then the fact that there will always be questions that we cannot answer need not prevent us from coming to an agreement about how to understand those aspects of our world which we share in common.   (Smolin 2001: 31)

There are more things in my humanism than the values in which I believe. However, I have chosen values as the focus of the 'something' in which I believe because I notice that my beliefs and values are particularly significant in structuring the ways in which I view myself, my relationships, the world and my being in the world. Whenever my values have changed this has had a quite profound impact on my life. Such change is not a frequent occurrence, but is somewhat seismic.

> Nihilism is the breakdown of the order of meaning, where all that was posited as a transcendent source of value in pre-Kantian metaphysics becomes null and void, where there are no cognitive skyhooks on which to hang a meaning for life. All transcendent claims for a meaning to life have been reduced to mere values …   (Critchley 1999: 11–12)

As I admitted above, I agree with the general thrust of Critchley's point, but here I wish to challenge the 'mere' in relation to values. Believing in my values is not a mere reduction of meaning for my life. Quite the converse: my values and their meaning for me are central to my sense of being. They define my existence.

Rorty has this to say:

> I have been urging in this book that we try not to want something which stands beyond history and institutions. The fundamental premise of the book is that a belief can still regulate action, can still be thought worth dying for, among people who are quite aware that this belief is caused by nothing deeper than contingent historical circumstances.
>
>   (1989: 189)

It follows from my nihilism that my values are in no way metaphysical statements. My beliefs and values do not, for me, exist *a priori*. They do not exist beyond the human condition. But they are nonetheless of central significance for me, they regulate my action. I am not sure if I would die for them.

I think that we, and by 'we' I mean my sense of the generality of people, have been deeply conditioned to think that we depend on external sources of validity in order to feel that what we believe or think is valid. Even if God is replaced by 'spirituality' there still seems residual reliance on some form of 'other' as a source of validation. Hierarchy is so thoroughly conditioned into us that there is a tendency to rely on external 'experts' or iconic figures not only for what to think but also for our sense of value as humans. I think that there are indications that such deference is diminishing and that with this diminution people are left to themselves to make their own minds up. I personally applaud such diminution. But this is a big responsibility and represents, I think, a great change in our sense of who we are and what we might become. Some of us are realising that we alone have responsibility for who we are and the kind of society which is possible. The so-called 'death of God' has wide ramifications. There is a loneliness and considerable challenge in accepting one's own responsibility for beliefs, values, meaning and agency.

> Once we enter the world for our temporary stay in it, there is no alternative but to try to decide what to believe and how to live, and the only way to do that is by trying to decide what is the case and what is right.   (Nagel 1997: 143)

Having said that, my values are based on what I think pertains to my sense of personal, relational, social and even political wellbeing. This rather vague notion of wellbeing is, in some respects, unpacked in my statements about my values. I need to be quite clear that I tend to extrapolate from my own sense of wellbeing to that of others. There is no necessary logic to this extrapolation: it's what I tend to do. I believe that my values are at least worth consideration – if only sceptical consideration – for adoption by others.

There are, of course, always possibilities for conflict between what I think is my wellbeing, and what others may think of my, and their, wellbeing. Conflicts of wellbeing are neither easily addressed nor easily resolved. In a sense, such conflict is what the problems of life are all about – personally, socially, politically and globally. The conflict becomes dangerous when dogma replaces empathy.

Of course I did not come to my values *ab initio*. They are the result of my living critically and thoughtfully in this particular society at this particular time and with my particular personal history. They are the result of what I think that I and others need in order to flourish personally and relationally, socially and politically. In familiar words: I tend to treat others as I would wish them to treat me. However, I have to recognise that others may have a different sense of what contributes to their wellbeing, and therefore their treatment of others (including me) will reflect their views as to what constitutes their own and others' wellbeing. That is fine by me as long as aspects of their search for wellbeing do not result in my death or suffering. And as long as it allows for dialogue.

There is a serious problem here for me in the elucidation of my values and in making them public. It is the charge of hypocrisy. That is, in so many respects my own standard of living and my sense of wellbeing depend on others whose work is under-rewarded and indeed whose lives are exploited in order to allow the wealth of the West to be maintained. I have no easy answer to this and when I focus on the issue it troubles me. It is a humbling reminder that I cannot act in total consistency with my espoused values. I am properly open to challenge on this issue. This awareness perhaps makes me more tolerant of others who also fail in the implementation of their espoused values. My commitment to conversation is also a commitment to being challenged, and that challenge includes a challenge to the validity of my values as well as to the extent to which I practise them.

I think that two things are likely to be the case: the first is that metanarratives in which we believe are permeated by values. Indeed, because metanarratives are ways of relating to the world, then the valuing process is endemic to our world-relating and people-relating. The second is that values can be identified, believed and acted upon without them necessarily being contingent upon a theological or metaphysical metanarrative. Self and values in the Enlightenment became nuanced. The simplistic polarities of theologically sourced good and evil were blurred, secularised and opened up to sceptical scrutiny. The nature of the interior life and the values which guide human action became the focus of scepticism. The genre of the novel, added to which were scientific and technological Enlightenment projects, created alternative interior possibilities which could be imagined, explored and emulated. Lodge even argues that the novel offers a complementary approach to scientific attempts at understanding consciousness (2002). One of the basic shifts which took place during the Enlightenment was that the self and values were problematised (see Porter 2000).

What follows is my latest attempt to clarify my values. I do not think that they necessarily depend for their validity, for me, on any particular metanarrative, although they do arise from my existence within the Judaeo-Christian tradition and within the Enlightenment project. They presuppose that I have a strong sense of my-self, of my identity. They presuppose that I have some degree of autonomy in relation to my actions and my choice of values. To that extent they may be seen as being located in the Enlightenment metanarrative. But they do not presume the isolated autonomy and rational self of the Enlightenment. They are culturally and relationally located. They are self-evidently embedded in a strong belief that people matter. Morality matters because morality is social as well as individual. Meaning matters. Beliefs are important. My philosophical friend of long standing suggests to me that my assumption that my beliefs and values 'matter' may be a moral metanarrative. There may well be something in this.

Grayling puts the matter with a simple directness:

> Humanity's sense of beauty, and decency, our power to love, our creativity – all the best things about us – belong to us, to human experience in the real world. They neither need, nor benefit from, some alleged connection with supernatural agencies of one kind or another. They are ours, just as much as the evil, stupidity, greed and cruelty which they oppose.
>
> (2001: 124)

The following list of values may seem rather obvious and relatively noncontroversial in a secular humanist model. That is as may be. The fact is that composing and reflecting on them took me a long time – and I found myself adding to and adapting them as I contemplated them, on and off, over months. One of the difficulties I had in verbalising my values is that some were so deeply embedded in my way of thinking/feeling that I was not very conscious of them. Some emerged into my consciousness only after considerable thought.

You may correctly infer that behind my statements of my values are whole swathes of my life, my relationships and my being in the world. They stand for an important summary of who and what I think I am. At least in my terms they are 'something' in which it is valid for me to believe.

The values in which I believe

> The supreme values in whose service man should live, especially when they were hard on him and exacted a high price – these social values were erected over man to strengthen their voice, as if they were commands of God, as 'reality', as true world, as a hope and future world. Now that the shabby origin of these values is becoming clear, the universe seems to have lost its value, seems 'meaningless' – but this is only a transitional stage.   (Nietzsche 1968: 10)

> Certainly we have values. They are implicit in what we do. Yet usually we do not make them explicit to ourselves or others.   (Oakley and Djikic 2002:103)

It took me longer than I expected to become aware of my values and that is because they are embedded in my way of being in the world. They provide the existential (and mostly unconscious) background to my being. Making the background into the foreground is difficult. What follows is what I have become aware of thus far. It is perhaps worth emphasising that I do not, cannot, know whether the values in which I believe are true. That is, I cannot know whether they are right in any ultimate sense. Nor can I know whether they are appropriate for all people. The values in which I believe give direction and purpose to my life and they are the basis for my relationships, political philosophy and notions of the kind of society, and indeed world, in which I would prefer to live. They represent the ideals to which I aspire but which I sometimes fail to achieve. I agree with Eagleton's position:

> If there is value at all, then it can only be in relation to ourselves, a relativity which threatens to undermine it.
>
> (2003: 209)

My values represent my beliefs about what makes for people's psychological, social and political interests and benefits in relationships, in communities and in society. Once again, my beliefs, values and meanings are closely intertwined.

They are not statements of certainty but statements of hope and of belief. They are not prescriptive in relation to human nature, but statements of possibilities which I believe to be desirable and around which there can be proper debate and possible agreement.

They reflect the kind of hope described by John Vidal (*The Guardian*, 11 November 2002) which was expressed in a gathering in Florence during the previous week. Under the title of 'Another Europe is Possible', the gathering consisted of '… 40,000 intellectuals, students, ecological and social activists, people representing the poorest and most marginalised, radical economists, concerned individuals, humanitarians, artists, culturalists, churches, scientists, and landworkers from a bewildering array of non-government groups and grass-roots social movements'.

This group is an expression of my values and the expression has practical implications. In other words, my values are grounded in what I perceive as their practical benefits and consequences for the enhancement of human experience. They are, to coin a phrase, value judgements. My value system is not based on the assumption of God as their basis although they share aspects of some religious values. My values are human, not divine. My values represent a form of optimism – optimism that human beings have possibilities for creative and fulfilling lives and for social, economic and political improvement. My values are statements of personal commitment and of options for human be-ing.

These, then, are my values.

Valuing respect for people, valuing my own and others' sense of wellbeing and dignity. This includes their right, or option, to choose to be different from me and for me to be different from them. I think that this is perhaps my primary value.

Part of this respect for people is valuing trust in relationships. Those relationships which have meant, and mean, most to me are those in which there is a high level of mutual trust. I have sometimes failed in this mutuality of trust and this failure has caused me some of my most unhappy experiences. Likewise when other people have betrayed a particularly high level of trust which I have invested in the relationship this too has caused considerable personal pain. I have come to believe that trust is the most important aspect in relationships which are affirming, accepting, supporting, developmental, challenging and enhancing. This is the case for personal and professional relationships. Trust is also necessary for political life and if this is lacking then cynicism and indifference set in. I think that there is work to be done on the relationship between trust and meaning – but not now. Trust is also a risky business.

> What we trustworthily declare must itself form the basis of our trusting each other, in the sense of providing the substance of living together.   (B. Williams 2002: 179)

Valuing a social and political order which treats people as having value in themselves and therefore recognising a moral dimension to the whole of life. Reference to 'the whole of life' does not imply a belief in God or in a sort of vaguely moral universe. It simply means that I believe that human relationships are essentially moral in that our behaviour inevitably impacts on the lives of others and that we are more or less aware of the fact of this impact if not of the details of the impact. My behaviour influences others' sense of wellbeing and dignity and is therefore a moral act. This includes a belief in the moral basis to organisations within which I and others work. I do not imply that such organisations actually behave necessarily in a beneficial (people enhancing) way, but that people in organisations cannot help but behave in a moral mode.

I value the recent moves to include animals in this valuing process, as they are capable of suffering pain and distress, so they ought to be treated with care. This issue has become an aspect of my valuing process.

I value equality of opportunity but issues around this are deeply complex for me. I applaud the efforts of this society to improve equality of opportunity. I value organisations in which there are policies, structures, processes, monitoring and review procedures and commitments to practise equality of opportunity. I value an organisational culture and style of relationships which actively, rather than rhetorically, values people. I note that even the recent Anglican acceptance of women priests (with some dissenters who refuse to accept their priestly validity) still excludes them from becoming bishops. Some other churches and religions do not allow women any formal status as religiously ordained leaders. Gay Christians are formally debarred from priestly office in many churches. My basic principle in relation to this is: equality of opportunity is the only basis for effective and empowering personal, relational, organisational, social and political functioning.

I value democratic principles of enfranchisement and represen-tation. For me, these principles of representation should include organisations in which I work, although many work organisations are self-evidently undemocratic in terms of the hierarchical structures and lack of transparency and accountability. They also do not allow the leaders to be elected and therefore removed. Religions seem to be particularly undemocratic and hierarchical as well as typically excluding women from access to all levels of the hierarchy.

In the context of democracy, I value conversation. Conversation involves two essential ingredients – speaking and listening – both of which are fundamental requirements for understanding and relating. As far as I can see it is only in democracies that open, challenging, developmental, critical conversations can take place. Conversation is about equality of opportunity.

I value being taken seriously and being treated with respect. This includes my valuing of being involved in decisions which are going to affect me in some important ways. If others act on my behalf I value the opportunity, to a greater or lesser extent, of being involved in consultation about that action.

I value consultation, communication and openness, but I reserve what I think is my right not to be open if I do not trust the other person.

I value my optimism – but I am certainly not a naïve optimist, heaven forbid! There's a great deal which seriously undermines my optimism. As I write an early draft we have just established the first Holocaust Memorial Day. Not a day of celebration of the unalloyed kindness of the human spirit. Hobsbawm asserts: 'The twentieth century was the most murderous in recorded history. The total number of deaths caused by or associated with its wars has been estimated at 187m, the equivalent of more than 10% of the world's population in 1913' (2002). A later draft takes place after 11 September 2001. I'm not sure why I put optimism at this point but, in terms of priorities, if my optimism collapsed then I sense that so would the rest of my values. My values themselves represent a form of optimism as I indicated above.

Valuing acceptance and being accepted by carefully chosen others. Part of being accepted is being listened to and listening. The mutuality of listening and being heard is very affirming and is not only the basis of psychotherapy but of becoming and being a confident human being. Bishop Berkeley (1685–1753 CE) stated that 'to be is to be perceived' (*esse est percipi*). He said this in the context of God being the ultimate perceiver of the world and of people. I think Berkeley had a sound (nontheological) point, but I would add that to be and to become we need to be heard.

Valuing rational discourse and by rational I mean critical, careful, detailed, informed, multifaceted discourse. I have some difficulty with the term 'rational'. Believing, as I do, that my thought is permeated by emotion and that the vast majority of my brain processes operate at a below conscious – and therefore below rational – level, I cannot be committed to a 'merely' rational assumption about the mind. I try to think clearly about issues, but those issues are not susceptible to being confined to my clear thinking. The world and the people in it are not such as to be able to fit into a particular way of *thinking* about them and therefore my attempts to be rational are only, and inevitably, partial ways of thinking.

I value my language and my careful use of language, but I have no evidence that the world can be fitted into my language without remainder. Some rationalists seem to make that assumption. I am not a rationalist *per se*. As I said earlier, I think and talk *about* things, I do not think and talk things *directly*. Language gives me a way of thinking and talking and the existence of the world gives me something to think and talk about. I value and enjoy my use of language.

I value my emotional life and the ways in which I try to incorporate my emotional awareness into my sense of who I am and how I relate to others. I also value being sensitive to others' emotions – not always with success. I have come to see that emotions are my basic responses to situations. Emotion cannot be deleted from my responses but it sometimes takes considerable efforts of self awareness to become aware of the emotional aspects of my responses. Emotions are indelible aspects of my being. Damasio's *The Feeling of What Happens: Body, emotion and the making of consciousness* (1999) helped me to appreciate, from a neurobiological point of view, the biological nature and ubiquity of emotions. My work in the area of counselling has helped me to appreciate the ubiquity of emotions in my subjectivity.

Likewise, I value my body and I keep appreciating that I am an embodied being. I try to avoid Cartesian dualism of mind and body, but this attempt to feel a sense of wholeness is not simple. However, constantly reminding myself of the effects of emotions on my reasoning and of the fact that my mind is embodied seems to be important to me. Shaw (in press) opens up new ways of understanding embodiment as he explores ways in which psychotherapists experience bodily changes during psychotherapy. I cannot be without my body (Humphrey 2002).

My awareness of Darwinian thought has led me to value the fact (my belief) that I am an animal and therefore part of the animal world. My attitudes to animals has changed since I took this awareness seriously.

I find that I value complexity and even confusion. I try to avoid oversimplification and glib reductionism. This could be seen as contradicting the minimalism of my nihilism. I see it as complementary not contradictory. I realise that I understand very little and even the little that I think I understand undergoes revision and review. My hold on my understanding and my sense of meaning is rather tenuous and sometimes it slips. Then I feel very vulnerable and even afraid. But generally my sense of confusion is the basis of development and enrichment.

I value my sense of curiosity and notice that this is a driving force in my life. It has proved to be a great advantage, but it has also involved me in some quite serious difficulties. Confusion, complexity and curiosity are linked for me. I also value taking some risks.

I value my ability to engage in critical reflexivity. In part this allows me to be self-critical and it seems to have the benefit that I can be more open in terms of trying to understand other people, situations and objects from a number of perspectives. To be critically reflexive I need to expose myself to a range of belief/faith positions which challenge my own. To be critically reflexive I need to be sceptical about my own beliefs and values and I need to expose myself to different systems in order to do this. Whatever I believe in, I am always a critical believer.

I value my ability to make decisions and to take actions. It seems that in spite of my commitment to critical reflexivity I am able to make decisions and to take actions which are generally consistent with my values. I say 'generally' because I am certainly not always consistent, and I recognise this. I find some decisions complicated to such an extent that I defer making them. I do not have a clear idea as to what total consistency would be like. I suspect that to assert the feasibility of total consistency leads to a form of dogma and intolerance of others who try to be consistent in ways which differ from my attempts at consistency. This way lies fundamentalism in its deeply pejorative sense. I do not like dogma and I have problems with dogmatic people.

I value my somewhat cryptic self-description of myself as a multiperspectival realist with idealist and constructivist tendencies – but when the chips are down, egocentric. That is to say: I am convinced that there is a reality independent of my perceiving it and that there are people to whom I relate. Not only do my own perceptions and constructions (ideas) of that complex reality and of complex people change over time (sometimes quite quickly) but other people construct different, and validly different, perceptions and ideas of that complex reality and of themselves and of others. However, because I am a self, albeit a self-in-relation, I have a tendency to egocentricity which makes me tend to privilege my own perspectives rather more strongly than those of others.

Another way of putting this is to say that I value my own experience, but I critique that experience myself and I look to close friends to provide criticism. Reading also provides me with many sources of experiential criticism as well as experiential enhancement. I do not assume that either my, or others', experiences are some mystical source of ultimate validity. My experience of being me and the experiences which construct that sense of being me are, indeed, constructed and can be deconstructed. I therefore think of my self as self-in-process. I do not know what a sense of self as having arrived would be like.

Valuing the integrity of the individual – but I'm not altogether clear what I mean by 'integrity'. I think that I mean something like: people should not be used as means to my ends or as means to ends generally. They have their own ends to which they are properly committed. They have a right to be who they are. I do not like feeling that I am being manipulated by others because it tends to undermine my sense of being clear as to what is happening to me. Sensing that I am being manipulated undermines my confidence in the other person and in myself. It undermines my own sense of integrity. I therefore try to accord the same kind of openness or straightforwardness to others – not with total success. I try not to manipulate others although I notice that I tend to want to do this if I feel that they are seeking to undermine me and not being open and fair. This is a complex area for me. In summary: I do not value being manipulated, controlled and dominated and I try not to manipulate, control and dominate others. I value open relationships, but do not always practise this openness.

I value scepticism, satire, dialogue and challenge.

I value intuition to some extent but I subject intuition to critical and sceptical scrutiny. My scepticism is what I crudely call my 'crap detector' which I apply to myself as well as to others.

Valuing human cultural and gender diversity. By this I mean that I do not believe that my own cultural conditioning is the only valid way of becoming an enculturated human being. However, I do value and enjoy some of the aspects of the broad Western metanarrative – for example, literacy, some degree of freedom of choice, being able to vote, the benefits of science and technology. I value the fact that gender and cultural diversity is slowly becoming affirmed. But of course, as I value democracy, there are limits to the nondemocratic (totalitarian) cultures which I can affirm in a wholehearted way.

Valuing the concept of 'progress' (note the inverted commas!). I think I mean something about becoming progressively aware of the complexities and diversities of life and of people. I do not mean progressively discovering what life is about or even making inevitable moral progress. I'm not at all sure what life is about – or even if it is 'about' anything in particular. Moral progress seems to me to be patchy but I think I see greater degrees of sensitivity to others' sufferings and others' needs in some aspects of social policy and action. Like trying to assess happiness in previous generations retrospectively, moral progress is difficult to be confident about. However, I value attempts made to make moral progress and I see the human rights movement, opposition to economic and cultural hegemony and glimmering indications of tolerance as forms of progress. Any sense of progress is always reversible. There is no accumulation of progress in the sense that it can be 'stored'. I have a strong feeling that the massive emphasis, in the West, on the individuality of consumerism militates against communal ethics and caring for 'the other'. The individualising of choice without awareness of social consequences dilutes a sense of social consequences of choice and draws on a very Western sense of the autonomous, un-social individual. I found myself in strong agreement with Rowan Williams in his chapter on 'Childhood and Choice' where he criticises the widespread notion of the child as a 'consumer' of goods and as one to be treated as a sexual object (2000: 11–52). Greater emphasis on the individual is not necessarily progress in social and communal terms. Neither is it progress for a powerful nation to dominate others either culturally or militarily. That is imperialism.

I value taking other people seriously and respecting their right to being treated in a dignified way. However, there are limits which I put on this and if I or others grossly transgress others' rights and wellbeing then I would expect my own and others' liberty to be restricted. Carefully scrutinised and challenged notions of justice are a consequence, for me, of taking people seriously. I object to the tendency to call the deaths of other human beings 'collateral damage'. This is a fundamental violation and denigration of their status as human beings. It is fundamentally disrespectful. As is the death penalty.

I value my ability to be committed to people and to projects, although my commitment is never such as to preclude scepticism. Nor does my commitment overlook my own needs in the relationship or the situation.

I value altruism not least because I live in a society, and a society can only operate on the basis that its members engage in actions which are in the public interest. Included in my valuing of altruism is a strong belief in the 'public sector'. Thatcher was wrong! Society does exist. A politically valued and properly resourced public sector, catering for the necessary aspects of a public life, not only meets the needs of the public and creates an awareness of belonging, social cohesion and responsibility, but it also provides opportunities for people to work in the public sector, thus giving opportunities for the exercise of altruism for the common weal. This altruism should not, however, be exploited by poor conditions of service and low pay. Work by the public for the public should be greatly valued. I therefore deplore any attempts to undermine the public sector. A thriving public sector also creates a proper sense of 'rights' as well as responsibilities. I want to emphasise the importance of a sense of belonging which a thriving and well-resourced public sector can help to create.

I value diversity – but there are limits to the diversity which I value because my valuing of diversity will include the values indicated above, for example respect for persons. So I cannot value a different value system which clearly does not value persons. I find it quite difficult to value people who surreptitiously or blatantly and cruelly disregard the value of others. But I value their right to fair treatment and justice. I also note how I myself have tendencies to ignore the negative effects on others of my middle-class and Western life style. I reluctantly conclude that, as a human being, I am by no means immune to perpetrating cruel and degrading treatment on others. In terms of living in the 'cosy' West this means that in some respects my life style is at the expense of others in the developing countries. The fact that this takes place at a distance from the exploited makes it easier for me to live with and to ignore for quite a lot of the time. It is these kinds of issues which make me hesitant about using the word 'integrity' too glibly.

I do not value systems which torture and kill people and engage in systematic humiliation. They do not attract my support whether this is done by my own country or others. I therefore do not value the export of armaments especially those which are designed to cause maximum damage to unsuspecting civilians.

Nearer home, I do not value, respect or trust organisations in which there are glaring and stressful mismatches between their people-valuing rhetoric (mission statements come to mind) and the way in which people are actually treated. I find myself being concerned about how easy it is to make grand statements as if the statements define the reality. I particularly resent grand statements which deem themselves to be beyond criticism. This happens in politics, religions, nationalisms and ironically in some forms of psychotherapy which seem to behave as if 'they' have the psychological truth about human nature and being.

I value flexibility and compromise. But there are limits to my willingness to compromise. I cannot stay long in close relationships in which there is no commitment to flexibility and compromise. I value reciprocity based on mutual respect. I therefore value diplomacy as a way of resolving international problems.

I value forgiveness as part of my attempt to be flexible and to be willing to compromise. Sacks has a nice phrase: 'In the face of tragedy, forgiveness is the counternarrative of hope' (2002: 179). He points out that forgiveness is a peculiarly human characteristic and is linked with our freedom to choose, freedom to be different from the past which constructed us. 'Forgiveness means that we are not destined endlessly to replay the grievances of yesterday. It is the ability to live with the past without being held captive by the past. At times it is the only path through the thickets of hate to the open spaces of coexistence' (2002: 179). I have both needed to be forgiven and needed to forgive if my relationships were to be productive, enhancing and developmental. I notice that in cases in which I have not been able to forgive a serious hurt, the relationship has usually ended or become superficial.

I value having people for whom I care and who care for me. Life without reciprocal caring would be bleak indeed. You may have noticed, as I just have, that I have not said that I value love. I do value commitment in relationships and I need relationships in which I can almost take commitment for granted – 'almost' but the commitment requires some kind of review and checking processes. Love is a slippery word. It can so easily be covertly manipulative and controlling. I suppose that when I say 'I love you', and if it is said with sincerity, it means that I have a deep sense of commitment to you. I care for you and I care about you. This caring was unconditional in relation to my children when they were totally dependent. I keep coming back to the importance of commitment. I also note the risks in commitment because of the inclusion of trust in commitment.

I value having friends with whom I can playfully and seriously explore deep and complex issues – intellectual, personal, existential – without having to come to any conclusions or having any conclusions forced upon me. Having mentioned friends – I value friendship. In particular I value friends who can allow me to change without rejecting me – and likewise me of them. A necessary ingredient of my friendships is that careful and reciprocal criticism is practised. My close friendships are very challenging relationships – but they are safe. I invest enormous trust in my friendships. My life would be emaciated without good friends. I have had close friends for most of my life. Those, few, times when they have been in short supply have been very difficult times for me. I enjoy a great sense of happiness and fun with my few, close friends.

I actually value something as simple as being courteous. I have sometimes been at the receiving end of discourtesy (and no doubt been discourteous myself). I really resent persistently discourteous people, particularly if I have to live with them or work with them. By courtesy I mean treating people with respect. Treating people fairly and preferably pleasantly. Treating people discourteously means treating them as if they don't matter. Part of my simple view of courtesy is to say 'please' and 'thank you'. These are not trivial for me.

I also value kindness: 'the quality of being friendly, generous and considerate' (*The New Oxford English Dictionary* 1998).

I value knowledge and learning. On balance I do not believe that ignorance is bliss, although I realise that what I think I know is extremely limited. Ignorance makes people very vulnerable – open to manipulation, exploitation and abuse. I pursue knowledge almost for its own sake, although I note that the knowledge which I pursue vigorously and over time has to do with the human condition and therefore to my own condition. Indeed I believe that all knowledge is about, or affects, the human condition in one way or another. Some knowledge which I pursue turns out to be disturbing in varying degrees. If a journey does not change me, why go on it?

I also value trying to be consistent in putting my values into practice, but I notice that I am not always consistent and this sometimes causes me to feel anxious and hypocritical. There are some tensions and even conflicts between my values and my thoughts, my feelings and my behaviour. I think that some of these are incapable of resolution and I suspect that total consistency is beyond me. This could sound like a cop-out.

I therefore value my belonging to the human species and I look upon all other people as my fellows. I do not value the description of some people as 'evil' for three reasons. First, I do not know what 'evil' might mean because I do not believe in any spiritual realm of 'good' and 'evil'. Secondly, the designation of some people as 'evil' seems to put them into a category other than human, and I deplore this. Thirdly, it is a totalising and utterly negative term. They are human. We are all simply human. There are moral categories of action but not moral categories of people. The historical and current tendencies to negatively categorise people inevitably leads to the oppression of those in the 'wrong' category. The very term 'evil' is redolent of a metanarrative which I do not accept – that of a way of categorising people which is spiritually and morally excluding and which makes it appropriate to punish and kill them. If we define people as 'other' (and additionally as 'evil') we seem to be able to treat them with degrees of cruelty which we would deplore if they treated us in this way. The more I have read and seen programmes about the ways in which people can torture and degrade their fellow human beings – and the more I understand the pressures which some were under to do this – the more I appreciate that I am unlikely to be immune from such behaviour under similar situations of coercive pressure. This is not to excuse brutal behaviour but I simply wish not to distance myself from such behaviour by presuming a 'holier' position of superiority. If other human beings could commit such atrocities then I am not immune. This a complex issue. I re-assert my rather banal statement that we are all human. There is a sense in which I 'own' rather than 'disown' the range of behaviour of which humanity is capable. That's what I mean when I say that we are all human. That is not a banal statement.

It may seem strange to say it, but I value a western sense of time – that is the idea that time is sort of linear. I say 'sort of' because the more I read and think about time the less I seem to know about it. Einstein's view on time really throws me as does my little knowledge of quantum mechanics. This much I have retained from a version of the 'traditional' Western metanarrative. I realise that 'Western' is merely local. I could not adopt a circular sense of my being in time without my whole sense of existential chronology being radically reviewed. At the moment I am not prepared to do that. By this I mean that I value the 'fact' (my belief) that my life had a beginning and it will have an end. I cannot ally myself with Nietzsche's notion of 'eternal recurrence' – a secular form of reincarnation.

Finally, I value my mortality. This may seem slightly odd. What I mean is that I value my belief that I was not before I was conceived and that I will not be after my death. I find that I feel liberated by this particular belief. My mortality is not, I think, a burden to me. Conversely I would not value immortality. The embodiment which I value is also the source of my mortality. My death is uniquely the experience from which I cannot learn by reflecting on my experience of it.

I note that there is no way known to me by which I could establish that the value statements above are grounded in any form of external reality (God, the cosmos, metaphysics or any such). Nor is it the case for me that my values indicate any spiritual dimension to life. I am not taken with current emphases on spirituality, not least because I do not know what the term means and I suspect that there is a new mystifying metanarrative in the air. I also sense that spirituality is a replacement for the loss of a personal version of God, a sort of pseudotheology (and perhaps cryptotheology) without the dogmatic trimmings. An attempt to persuade one's self that there is order, purpose and meaning rather than chaos. That may seem offensive or puzzling to some, but it's what I think. Howard takes a different view of spirituality and indeed of spirituality as a potential metanarrative:

> Can romantic emotion and classical reason be integrated into a larger, more embracing apprehension of the universe? My own feeling is that they can, which may take me a long way from postmodern fragmentalism. Neither do I think that such integration requires an easy consensus, or 'final synthesis'. I persist in the felt sense that spirituality does not have to edge us towards escapism, dogmatic theology or irrationalism. Science itself, I would suggest, leads us to a sense of awe, wonder, tentative enquiry and a basic faith that 'grand narratives' are possible and that, however many perspectives we may take on it, there is one universe to be shared rather than endless incommensurable private worlds … I hear a symphony not a cacophony.   (2000: 373–74)

I actually agree with Howard about the 'one universe to be shared' and about awe, wonder and tentative enquiry, and at the same adopt my multiperspectival realism with constructivist tendencies in relation to the one (or more) universes. I mean that the 'universe' seems, in modern physics as well as in diverse cultures and even scientific subcultures, to be capable of being perceived from different perspectives and given different meanings. Reality isn't only or simply a homogeneity to be discovered but a multiplicity to be invented. There is, I suspect, no single truth. Thus I find it difficult to hear a 'symphony' because I hear diverse constructions – different marches to different musics. I can generally agree with his use of the term 'postmodern fragmentation' but I have a different take on the value of fragmentation. For me it involves the valuing of diversity. It also poses in stark relief the problem of meaning.

I am not in a position to compel others to accept my values. Indeed, compulsion would contravene my first value of respect for people. In any serious dialogue with those who differ from me I only have the power of persuasion. But that's all right, because persuasion is based on respect for persons – respecting their right to differ from me in fundamental respects. I only hope that if the worst came to the worst they might also respect my right to differ from them. Dogmatic orthodoxists would be unlikely to respect any of my 'rights' or indeed my values. I don't think that it would be possible for me to have a dialogue with dogmatists.

You will appreciate my meaning when I say that to a large extent my values create my narrative. They are the existential 'glue' of my narrative and of my life. They plot the main points of my own sense of significance and dignity and of the significance and dignity which I try to accord to others. Of course, there's more to my narrative than my values (memories, aspirations, events, sense of place, culture, my age, gender, nationality, activities to which I am committed, contexts in which I feel that I belong, things which 'belong' to me, relationships, the framework which I try to give to my life and so on) but I do not think that I could make any meaning of these other aspects of my narrative if I lacked a value system.

From another perspective, I think that the significance of these other aspects of my narrative would change if there were to be a significant change to my values. Indeed this actually did take place when I gave up believing in God and then when I gave up believing in scientific reductionism. Previous events and meanings in my life came to be viewed differently by me after I gave up my theological beliefs. I notice that my past is flexible because I can have flexible perspectives on it. Even to talk of past as an 'it' is grossly misleading. Past is process and past is existentially and biologically present in my brain and body. Traumas to my brain change my memory and therefore my history. I also notice that I developed a greater sense of valuing myself after I had ceased to believe in God. This may seem paradoxical to some, but true for me. It seems as if my sense of my being as only having value because of my dependence on God diminished my sense of being valuable in my own right.

My values have a deep sense of existential ontology for me – that is in some sense they create my sense of being in the world. They inform my present (which is always process), my changing view of my past (so my past is process) and my sense of my future, which is always changing and basically unknowable. The fact that I am getting older is a very significant aspect of my self as a process in the constructing.

I don't see how we can avoid having some form of values. They are endemic to human be-ing and human relatedness. They are not, for me, indicative of a value basis to the universe. I live with my values. I can change them. They define my being and my relatedness. All metanarratives are permeated by values.

What I *do not* believe is quite succinctly put by John Polkinghorne, Anglican Priest, formerly particle physicist and formerly President of Queen's College, Cambridge:

> Belief in the existence of God, as defined by concepts that would be held in common by the three great monotheistic world faiths, Judaism, Christianity and Islam, means that reality makes total sense and that the key explanatory principle needed for understanding is the recognition that the world is the creation of a divine agent. This, in turn,

implies four statements that need to be defended: there is
a Mind behind the order of the world; a Purpose behind
its unfolding history; the One thus revealed is worthy of
worship; and God is the ground of an everlasting hope.

(Polkinghorne 2002: 6)

I do not believe in any of these four statements. Nor do I believe
that there is evidence for them which I would find persuasive.
I can see how they are attractive for some people in terms of
creating an apparently divine – and therefore external and
externally validated – basis for the meaning of life.

In an earlier article Polkinghorne states:

> The encounter with the sacred, to which the world faith
> traditions testify, is a meeting with the divine presence. The
> coherence and persuasiveness of theism depends partly on
> acknowledging the rich and many layered nature of the
> reality within which we live. The same event can be both
> an occurrence in the physical world, a carrier of beauty,
> a challenge to moral decision and an encounter with the
> sacred. For the religious believer, an occasion of worship will
> often have all these dimensions. Belief in God ties together
> these levels of experience. God is worthy of worship because
> God is ultimately the ground of the good, the true and the
> beautiful.   (2001)

I can accept the notion of *the many layered nature of reality* but
after that I part company. After all, Polkinghorne was a member
of the Church of England Doctrine Commission which believes,
as a matter of doctrine, that 'hell is a state of non-being indicating
the very worst condition that a person could be in'. This is quite
contrary to Buddhists who believe that non-being is nirvana.
Polkinghorne's belief in hell and in a God who can apparently
accede to this belief in hellish non-being as a 'worst condition'
offends my humanistic value system. I also note: 'Virginia Woolf
once wrote that all accounts of life are misleading because states
of non-being are impossible to describe' (Rose 2003: 72) which
at least challenges Polkinghorne's confidence about 'worst

condition'. If I did ever come to believe in a God, this God would not have moral attributes which are less than those of my current humanism. What I appreciate about Polkinghorne's position is that he is able to put it succinctly and with great clarity. The essential content of his metanarrative is clear. There are aspects of it with which I agree.

Polkinghorne's clarity suggests that it is useful to try to stipulate what are the essential features of one's metanarrative. The following is a possible model for doing this:

1   What might be a label for your metanarrative?
2   Make it clear that your metanarrative is a belief position, not a truth position, by stating what you believe to be the case.
3   Avoid tendencies to slip from 'believing' to 'knowing'.
4   Provide as much relevant evidence as possible to support your metanarrative. You may need to explain why you deem some evidence as 'relevant'.

While preparing this section on values I have wondered if it is the case that I do not have a metanarrative and whether I simply have a narrative. My long-term friend and philosophical discussant suggests that I do have a metanarrative. Maybe so. If so, I think it would be a minimal metanarrative of moral mattering. I like the alliteration and I owe the notion of 'moral mattering' to my friend. Another way of accessing my metanarrative is to consider my credo.

Such a metanarrative, if that is what it is, simply asserts that human beings matter and that this mattering is something without which I could not imagine being human. It allows for diversity. It is not imperialistic – except that I might argue that it would be a 'good thing' if all human beings could accept that they and therefore others matter in a moral sense. They matter enough for them not to be arbitrarily, wilfully or officially killed. I can see that all my values flow from this sense of mattering. It is not a statement of a universal 'how things are' but a statement of a universal aspiration – how I would like things to be. If it was a statement of 'how things are', then it would be nearer to Polkinghorne's view of God. To this extent it is similar to the moral pragmatism of Rorty who believes that it is universally the case that human beings should not be subjected to gratuitous pain or to humiliating or degrading treatment. He discusses these issues in *Contingency, irony and solidarity* (1989). There are echoes here of the Universal Declaration of Human Rights. Universal, not in the sense of them being universally present in the human condition, but a universal aspiration (see Klug 2000). Even this notion of a universal aspiration is not the case. Some countries have refused to sign up to them and some countries were explicitly excluded from their construction.

It is difficult to arrive at consensus on universality.

My inconclusive conclusion

'Do you believe in God?'
    'Would you rephrase that question, please?'
                                            (Porter 2001: 76)

God's ominous silence, the loss of heaven, makes that world more precious at the very moment that it highlights its perishability.   (Eagleton 2003: 209)

Frances: We don't know anything, do we?
Madeleine: No, not much.
Frances: We think we're being clever, but it's way beyond us.
    Most anyone can hope for is to avoid being stupid.
                                            (Hare 2002: 39)

I therefore conclude by asserting that I believe in nothing and something. I am a nihilist in the sense that I do not believe that 'life' has any meaning other than that which 'we' give it. I believe in something because I believe that the human species has a wide range of potentials, one of which is that of trying to develop values which will enable us to live together in creative and enhancing rather destructive and demeaning ways.

I feel I have to say both of these things at once: I believe in nothing and something. It's difficult to escape from dualism.

It has been a considerable challenge to articulate my own position in as clear and honest a way as I can manage. I suggest that you might make an attempt at putting your own beliefs/ values position into print. Writing one's position down helps to avoid waffle – I hope.

> The line of thought common to Blumenberg, Nietzsche,
> Freud and Davidson suggest that we try to get to the point
> where we no longer worship anything, where we treat
> nothing as quasi divinity, where we treat everything – our
> language, our conscience, our community – as a product
> of time and chance. To try to reach this point would be, in
> Freud's words, to 'treat chance as worthy of determining our
> fate'.   (Rorty 1989: 22)

Who put me on the list of human beings? Nobody did. It's
chance. I am just on it – like Brodsky. But while I'm on the list I
am capable of rising to heights as well as plumbing depths.

I am simply human.

And finally, back to Macbeth:

> A tale told by an idiot … signifying nothing.

But I am that —— idiot, and it's my —— tale!!! (expletives
deleted).

So that's OK then.

References

Ashman K.M. and Baringer P.S. (eds.), 2001, *After The Science Wars* (London: Routledge).

Aunger R. (ed.), 2000, *Darwinizing Culture: The status of memetics as a science* (Oxford: Oxford University Press).

Barrow J.D., 2001, *The Book of Nothing* (London: Vintage).

Bracken P., 2002, *Trauma: Culture, Meaning and Philosophy* (London: Whurr).

Brandom R.B. (ed.), 2000, *Rorty and His Critics* (Oxford: Blackwell).

Cetina K.K., 1999, *Epistemic Cultures: How the sciences make knowledge* (London: Harvard University Press).

Chomsky N., 2002, *9–11* (New York: Seven Stories Press).

Clocksin W.F., 1998, 'Artificial intelligence and human identity' in J. Cornwell (ed.), *Consciousness and Human Identity* (Oxford: Oxford University Press), 101–21.

Conte R., 2000, 'Memes through (social) minds' in Aunger R. (ed.), *Darwinizing Culture: The status of memetics as a science* (Oxford: Oxford University Press), 83–119.

Cornwell J. (ed.), 1998, *Consciousness and Human Identity* (Oxford: Oxford University Press).

Critchley S., 1999, 'Introduction' in S. Critchley and W.R. Schroeder (eds.), *A Companion to Continental Philosophy* (Oxford: Blackwell), 1–17.

—— and Schroeder W.R. (eds.), 1999, *A Companion to Continental Philosophy* (Oxford: Blackwell).

Damasio A., 1999, *The Feeling of What Happens: Body, emotion and the making of consciousness* (London: Heinemann).

Davidson D., 2000, 'Truth Rehabilitated' in R.B. Brandom (ed.), *Rorty and His Critics* (Oxford: Blackwell), 65–74.

de Botton A., 2000, *The Consolations of Philosophy* (London: Hamish Hamilton).

Dennett D.C., 1995, *Darwin's Dangerous Idea: Evolution and The Meanings of Life* (Harmondsworth: Penguin Books).

—— , 2003, *Freedom Evolves* (London: Penguin Books).

D'Isanto L., 1999, 'Introduction' in G. Vattimo, *Belief* (Cambridge: Polity Press), 1–17.

Eagleton T., 2003, *Sweet violence: the idea of the tragic* (Oxford: Blackwell).

Farrell F.B., 1996, *Subjectivity, Realism and Postmodernism. The Recovery of the World in Recent Philosophy* (Cambridge: Cambridge University Press).

Ferrari M., 2002, 'Editorial', *Journal of Consciousness Studies*, Vol. 9, Nos. 9–10, 1–10.

Fromm E., 2001, *The Fear of Freedom* (London: Routledge).

Fuller S., 2001, 'The reenchantment of science' in K.M. Ashman and P.S. Baringer (eds.), *After The Science Wars* (London: Routledge), 183–208.

Genova J., 1995, *Wittgenstein: A Way of Seeing* (London: Routledge).

Gould S.J., 1999, *Rocks of Ages: Science and Religion in the Fullness of Life* (New York: The Ballantine Publishing Group).

Gray J., 2002, *Straw Dogs: Thoughts on humans and other animals* (London: Granta Books).

Grayling A.C., 2001, *The Meaning of Things: Applying Philosophy To Life* (London: Weidenfeld and Nicholson).

Greenfield S., 2000, *The Private Life of the Brain* (London: Allen Lane/ The Penguin Press).

Hare D., 2002, *The Breath of Life* (London: Faber and Faber).

Hatfield G., 2003, *Routledge Philosophy Guidebook to Descartes and the Meditations* (London: Routledge).

Heath G., 2000, 'A constructivist attempts to talk to the field', *The International Journal of Psychotherapy*, Vol. 5, No. 1, 11–35.

—— , 2002a, 'Philosophy and Psychotherapy: Conflict or Co-operation?', *The International Journal of Psychotherapy*, Vol. 7, No. 1, 13–52.

—— , 2002b, 'Does a Theory of Mind Matter? The myth of totalitarian scientism', *The International Journal of Psychotherapy*, Vol. 7, No. 3, 185–220.

Hobsbawm E., 2002, 'War and Peace', *The Guardian*, 23 February 2002.

Hobson P., 2002, *The Cradle of Thought: Exploring the Origins of Thinking* (London: Macmillan Press).

Howard A., 2000, *Philosophy for Counselling and Psychotherapy* (London: Macmillan Press).

Humphrey N., 2002, *The Mind Made Flesh: Essays from the Frontiers of Psychology and Evolution* (Oxford: Oxford University Press).

Huntington S., 1996, *The Clash of Civilizations and the Remaking of World Order* (New York: Simon and Schuster).

Jacques M., 2002, *The Guardian*, 5 October 2002.

Klug F., 2000, *Values in a Godless Age: The Story of the United Kingdom's New Bill of Rights* (London: Penguin).

Kornblith H., 2002, *Knowledge and its Place in Nature* (Oxford: Oxford University Press).

LaBerge S., 2002, 'What is a dream?' in H. Swain (ed.), *Big Questions in Science* (London: Jonathan Cape), 55–67.

Lakoff G. and Johnson M., 1999, *Philosophy in The Flesh: the embodied mind and its challenge to Western thought* (New York: Basic Books).

Lodge D., 2002, *Consciousness and The Novel* (London: Secker and Warburg).

Longino H.E., 2002, *The Fate of Knowledge* (Princeton: Princeton University Press).

Lyotard J.-F., 1979 (trans. 1984), *The Postmodern Condition: A Report on Knowledge* (Manchester: Manchester University Press).

Maddox J., 2002, 'Preface' in H. Swain (ed.), *Big Questions in Science* (London: Jonathan Cape), viii–xii.

Nagel T., 1986, *The View from Nowhere* (Oxford: Oxford University Press).

——, 1997, *The Last Word* (Oxford: Oxford University Press).

——, 1999, *Other Minds: Critical Essays, 1969–1994* (paperback edition, Oxford: Oxford University Press).

Nietzsche F., 1968, *Will to Power* (New York: Vintage Books).

——, 1974, *The Gay Science* (trans. W. Kaufmann; New York: Random House).

O'Neill O., 2002, *A Question of Trust* (Cambridge: Cambridge University Press).

Oatley K. and Djikic M., 2002, 'Emotions and Transformation: Varieties of Experience of Identity', *Journal of Consciousness Studies*, Vol. 9, Nos. 9–10, 97–116.

Papineau D., 2002, *Thinking about Consciousness* (Oxford: Oxford University Press).

Phillips A., 1999, *Darwin's Worms* (London: Faber and Faber).

——, 2001, *Houdini's Box: On The Arts of Escape* (London: Faber and Faber).

——, 2002, *Equals* (London: Faber and Faber).

Pinker S., 2002, *The Blank Slate: the modern denial of human nature* (London: Allen Lane/The Penguin Press).

Polkinghorne J., 2001, 'Only the hand of God could have conjured up the mind of mankind', *Times Higher Education Supplement*, 15 June 2001.

——, 2002, 'Does God exist?' in H. Swain (ed.), *Big Questions in Science* (London: Jonathan Cape), 6–10.

Porter P., 2001, *Max is Missing* (London: Picador).

Porter R., 2000, *Enlightenment: Britain and the Creation of the Modern World* (London: Allen Lane/The Penguin Press).

Ramachandran V.S. and Blakeslee S., 1999, *Phantoms in the Brain* (London: Fourth Estate).

Richards J.R., 2000, *Human Nature After Darwin: A Philosophical Introduction* (London: Routledge).

Rees M., 2001, *The Guardian*, 29 December 2001.

Rorty R., 1989, *Contingency, irony, and solidarity* (Cambridge: Cambridge University Press).

——, 2000, 'Universality and truth' in R.B. Brandom (ed.), *Rorty and His Critics* (Oxford: Blackwell), 1–30.

Rose H. and Rose S. (eds.), 2000, *Alas, Poor Darwin: Arguments Against Evolutionary Psychology* (London: Jonathan Cape).

Rose J., 2003, *On Not Being Able To Sleep: Psychoanalysis and the Modern World* (London: Chatto and Windus).

Rose S., 2002, 'What is life about?' in H. Swain (ed.), *Big Questions in Science* (London: Jonathan Cape), 221–31.

Ruse M., 2002, 'Are we still evolving?' in H. Swain (ed.), *Big Questions in Science* (London: Jonathan Cape), 187–97.

Ruthven M., 2002, *A Fury for God: the Islamist attack on America* (London: Granta Books).

Sacks J., 2002, *The Dignity of Difference. How to avoid the clash of civilizations* (London: Continuum).

Schroeder W.R., 1999, 'Afterword' in S. Critchley and W.R. Schroeder (eds.), *A Companion to Continental Philosophy* (Oxford: Blackwell), 613–38.

Scott C.E., 1999, 'Nietzsche' in S. Critchley and W.R. Schroeder (eds.), *A Companion to Continental Philosophy* (Oxford: Blackwell), 153–61.

Shaw R., in press, *The Embodied Psychotherapist: The Therapist's Body Story* (London: Brunner–Routledge).

Smolin L., 2001, *Three Roads to Quantum Gravity: A new understanding of space, time and the universe* (London: Phoenix).

Sokal A. and Bricmont J., 1998, *Intellectual Impostures* (London: Profile Books).

Spinelli E., 2001, *The Mirror and The Hammer: Challenges to Therapeutic Orthodoxy* (London: Continuum).

Swain H. (ed.), 2002, *Big Questions in Science* (London: Jonathan Cape).

Tarnas R., 1996, *The Passion of the Western Mind* (London: Pimlico).

Taylor M.C., 1987, *Erring: A Postmodern A/theology* (Chicago: University of Chicago Press).

Trigg R., 2002, *Philosophy Matters* (Oxford: Blackwell).

Varela F.J., Thompson E. and Rosch E., 1996, *The Embodied Mind: Cognitive Science and Human Experience* (Cambridge, MA and London: MIT Press).

Vattimo G., 1999, *Belief* (Cambridge: Polity Press).

Weller P. (ed.), 2001, *Religions in the UK* (3rd edition, Derby: The Multi-faith Centre, University of Derby, in association with the Interfaith Network for the United Kingdom).

Williams B., 2002, *Truth and Truthfulness* (Woodstock, Oxfordshire: Princeton University Press).

Williams R., 2000, *Lost Icons. Reflections on Cultural Bereavement* (Edinburgh: T. and T. Clark).

——, 2002, *Writing in the dust. Reflections on 11th September and its aftermath* (London: Hodder and Stoughton).

Wilson E.O., 1998, *Consilience: the unity of knowledge* (London: Little, Brown and Company).

Wittgenstein L., 1953, *Philosophical Investigations* (2nd edition, Oxford: Blackwell).

Index

9/11. *See* terrorism

abuse, 108
acceptance, 99
accountability, 46, 73, 79, 98
Afghanistan, 1
afterlife, 85
agency, 14, 18, 66, 91
al-Qaeda, 1
altruism, 19, 104
America. *See* United States of
    America
Anglicanism, 16, 23, 24, 33, 97, 112
anxiety, 3, 29, 48, 87, 108
apikoras. *See* heresy
arms & armaments, 1, 105
artefacts, 54, 78, 84
aspirations, 60, 111, 115
atheism, 44
Augustine, Saint (354–430), 39, 48
authority, 15, 19, 22, 25, 26, 28, 31,
    32, 48
autism, 84
autonomy, 62, 73, 80, 83, 93, 103
awareness, 1, 20, 22, 32, 39, 70, 71,
    74, 79, 81, 92, 99, 100, 103, 104
axis of evil, 20, 21, 86

Bali, 2
belief(s)
    about meaning of life, 40
    about the world, 42
    acceptance of, 15
    affirmation of, 17
    and actions, 18
    and free will, 74
    and identity, 70
    and knowledge, 8, 12, 16, 24, 25,
        31, 32, 69
    and meaning, 4, 61, 87, 95
    and myths, 3, 4, 23
    and orthodoxy, 15
    and reality, 76
    and religion, 16
    and subjectivity, 70
    and symbols, 42
    and truth, 70, 114
    and values, 1–3, 5, 8, 13, 18, 21, 23,
        34, 38, 43, 64–67, 73, 80, 81, 87,
        89–91, 93, 95, 101, 117
    as habits of action, 76
    as need for meaning, 86
    as negative theology, 44
    authenticity of, 46
    change in, 33, 53, 71, 80
    clarification of, 5, 17
    compelling but false, 30
    confidence in, 39
    confusion with truth, 47
    correct, 31, 32
    culturally constructed, 78
    definition of, 15, 16
    demarcations in, 29
    dogmatic, 21
    effect of, 18, 90
    error of, 25, 26
    exposure to other, 101
    fallible, 70

function of, 32
high profile of, 18
humanistic, 17, 33, 34, 42, 89
impact of science on, 59
impact on others, 87
importance of, 22, 93
important aspects of, 23
imposed, 69
in benefits of conversation, 30
in evolution, 55
in God, 2–4, 16, 30, 34, 38, 45, 52,
    59, 60, 61, 71, 73, 81, 96, 112–14,
    117
in metaphysics, 83
in moral basis to organisations, 97
in public sector, 104
in science, 59, 62
indicators, 17
influence of science on, 44
intense, 69
invention of, 44
inventions, 69
Jewish, 26
justification of, 76
longevity of, 70
necessity of, 13
nihilistic, 43, 68
optimistic, 65
origins of, 30, 33, 34, 64, 76
orthodox, 70
personal, 6, 39, 42, 44, 53, 59, 62,
    66–68, 70, 71, 75, 76, 78, 87, 89,
    90, 93, 99, 100, 101, 109, 117
plurality of, 30
reason for, 12
religious, 3, 5, 20–22, 24, 29, 31,
    33, 34, 45, 46, 58, 63, 69, 113
removal of, 59
responsibility for, 91
self, 55, 71
significance of, 43
source of, 64
statements, 9, 17, 47, 63, 95
systems, 2, 13, 18, 20, 22, 24, 31,
    32, 47, 68, 75, 86, 101
that people matter, 93

theological, 70, 112
validity of, 33, 39, 42
value of, 43
believing
    community of, 17
    modes of, 64
    versus knowing, 12, 16, 46, 47, 63,
        114
belonging, 3, 4, 31, 104, 105, 108
Bible, 25
biology, 5, 51, 54–56, 58, 64, 65, 100,
    112
black energy, 57
black holes, 57
black matter, 57
blasphemy, 56
brevity of life, 52, 59
Buddhism, 29, 113
Burnet, Rev. Thomas (1635–1715),
    52

Camus, Albert (1913–60), 37, 42
Canterbury, Archbishop of, 24, 25,
    31, 83
capitalism, 85
Carey, George, 31. *See also*
    Canterbury, Archbishop of
Cartesian philosophy. *See* Descartes
Catholicism, 2
causality, 59
challenges, 4, 11, 21, 54, 59, 90–92,
    101, 102, 113, 117
charity, 17
childhood, 41
children, 15, 17, 19, 56, 84, 104, 107
choice, 42, 55, 60, 62–65, 73–75, 83,
    93, 96, 103, 104, 106
Christianity, 2, 12, 13, 16, 18, 20, 23,
    24, 27, 52, 53, 59, 68, 97, 112
chronologies, 16, 109
Church of England Doctrine
    Commission, 113
Church Society, 23–25
cloning, 56, 66
commandments, 31

commitment, 29, 32, 43, 92, 96, 97, 101, 104, 106, 107
community, 2, 3, 16, 17, 21, 27, 95, 118
complexity, 2, 8, 54, 61, 63, 64, 67, 70, 73, 87, 97, 100–02, 107, 109
compromise, 106
conditioning, 90, 103
confidence, 12, 24, 60, 66, 67, 70, 73, 99, 102, 103, 113
    in beliefs, 39
confusion, 3, 17, 29, 47, 64, 100, 101
conscience, 9, 118
consistency, 9, 92, 101, 108
consumerism, 56, 103, 104
control, 6, 7, 32, 56, 62, 102, 107
conversation, 7, 8, 15, 26, 28–32, 78, 92, 98, 99. *See also* debate, dialogue
cosmic absurdity, 60
cosmic age, 52
cosmic meaning, 52, 71
cosmic mind/soul, 58
cosmology, 38, 52, 54, 57
cosmos, 52, 75, 110
courtesy, 107
Creationism, 54, 66
credos, 6, 9, 12, 33, 114
creeds, 6, 16, 17, 21, 27, 62
cruelty, 89, 93, 105, 109
crusades, 20, 31
cultural
    artefacts, 78, 84
    constructs, 58
    context, 73
    diversity, 103
    forms of language, 81
    hegemony, 103
    identity, 15
    images, 45
    legitimacy, 19
    norms, 82
    values, 61
culture, 5, 18, 33, 42, 64, 65, 78, 97, 111
cultures, 33, 43, 44, 60, 65, 74, 103, 111

curiosity, 7, 100, 101
cynicism, 96

Darwin, Charles (1809–82), 13, 44, 53–56, 66, 75, 100
death, 1, 4, 19, 28, 29, 37, 46, 48, 60, 69, 75, 92, 104, 109, 110
debate, 22, 25, 29, 33, 34, 73, 95. *See also* conversation, dialogue
democracy, 20, 22, 62, 97, 98, 103
Derby, 11
Descartes, 41, 51, 54, 68, 73, 100
destiny, 9
dialogue, 15, 27–32, 92, 102, 111. *See also* conversation, debate
difference, 15, 20, 24, 26–29, 34, 64, 87
dignity, 26–29, 34, 66, 87, 96, 97, 104, 111
diplomacy, 106
discourtesy, 107
disease, 1
diversity, 20, 29, 66, 87, 103, 105, 111, 114
divine
    agency, 112
    basis for meaning of life, 113
    being, 7, 46
    cause, 71
    creativity, 54
    imperative, 20
    norm, 72
    origins of life, 56
    presence, 113
    punishment, 33
    sense of origin, 2
    source of religious beliefs, 34
    teleology, 53
    truth, 39
    values, 95
divinity, 24, 25, 118
divorce, 48
DNA, 55, 57
dogmatism, 7, 8, 13, 18, 21, 23, 29, 30, 35, 44, 69, 87, 91, 101, 110, 111
dreams, 80, 81

dualism, 12, 42, 73, 100, 117

egocentricity, 101, 102
Einstein, Albert (1879–1955), 44, 62, 109
embodiment, 6, 40, 43, 64, 77, 79, 81, 100, 109
emotion, 3, 53, 65, 66, 75, 80, 84, 99, 100, 110
empathy, 80, 91
empiricism, 34, 40, 51, 53, 61, 67
enfranchisement, 97
England, 24, 25, 107
Enlightenment, 12, 13, 33, 38, 43, 92, 93
epistemology, 12, 38, 43, 47, 64, 68, 69, 74
equality, 97, 98
essentialism, 84
ethics, 2, 37, 54, 89, 103
Evangelism, 31
evidence, 2, 3, 16, 39, 47, 48, 51–53, 55, 61, 62, 65, 66, 70, 99, 113, 114
evil, 3, 18–22, 85, 87, 89, 92, 93, 108
  axis of, 21, 86
evolution, 13, 54, 55, 57, 59, 66
exclusion, 31, 32, 87, 98, 108, 115
existentialism, 5, 6, 11, 16, 34, 39, 44, 48, 52, 60–62, 68–70, 73, 75, 84, 94, 107, 109, 111, 112
exploitation, 8, 92, 105, 108
extermination, 22
external
  basis for meaning of life, 113
  design, 60
  form of meaning, 86
  given, 84
  meaning, 3, 52
  meaning of life, 43
  reality, 110
  sources of meaning, 14, 45, 48, 74
  sources of purpose, 3
  sources of religious beliefs, 34
  sources of validity, 90
  validation, 47, 113
  view, 71

world, 6, 16, 40

faith, 1, 7, 26–32, 38, 39, 53, 84, 101, 110, 113
faiths, 1, 11, 27, 31, 32, 112
famine, 1
fatwa, 31
fideism, 12, 44, 45, 47, 69
fideology, 47
flexibility, 78, 106, 112
forgiveness, 46, 106
free will, 72–74
freedom, 3, 20–22, 29, 48, 54, 56, 65, 73, 74, 83, 103, 106
Freud, Sigmund (1856–1939), 39, 44, 75, 77, 118
friends & friendship, 5, 6, 11, 23, 67, 93, 102, 107, 114
fundamentalism, 18–20, 25, 30, 101

genetics, 55, 56, 57
geology, 52, 53
God, 28. *See also* belief in God
  as basis of value system, 95
  as normative value, 72, 73
  as shorthand, 6, 17
  as source of meaning, 14, 84
  as source of purpose in life, 13
  as source of values, 110
  attributes of, 2
  authority of, 25
  awareness of, 32
  blessing of, 20
  child of, 68
  commands of, 94
  death of, 37, 46, 47, 60, 82, 91
  dependence on, 80, 82
  existence of, 46, 70, 82
  form of, 30, 34
  ground of everlasting hope, 113
  handiwork of, 56
  humanity as pinnacle of creation, 54
  is death, 46
  loss of, 48, 71
  mentions of, 23

narcissistic, 20
notion of, 2
obedience to, 20
omniscience of, 99
on their side, 25
ownership of, 34
personal, 17
relevance to, 75
replaced by science, 62, 66
replaced by spirituality, 90
revelation of, 27, 32
silence of, 117
speaking to mankind, 27
truth about, 26
used as ultimate authority, 19
version of, 25
view of, 115
will of, 18, 19, 43
word of, 25
gods, 29, 75
government, 9
gravity, 57, 74

hegemony, 103
heresy, 23, 24, 26, 28, 31–33, 66
heteronomy, 80, 83
Holocaust, 98
homogeneity, 82, 111
homosexuality, 24, 97
hubris, 48
human
    action, 92
    activity, 7, 74
    beings, 1, 21, 42, 45, 46, 55, 65, 82,
        83, 87, 96, 99, 104, 105, 109, 114,
        115, 118
    belief/meaning systems, 68
    beliefs, 74
    body, 7, 56
    characteristics, 106
    choice, 64
    condition, 8, 30, 34, 60, 90, 108,
        115
    culture, 64
    diversity, 103

existence, 15, 22, 32, 68, 72, 84, 96,
    106, 112
experience, 12, 60, 89, 93, 95
feeling more, 71
goals and commitments, 43
identity, 80
issues, 54
knowing, 12
knowledge, 13, 41, 83
less than, 22
life, 52, 83
meaning, 46
mind, 40, 43, 51, 58–60, 62–64
more than, 49
nature, 5, 62, 64, 95, 106
norms, 44
potential, 49
project, 84
reason, 64
relatedness, 4, 23, 112
relationships, 96
reproduction, 55
rights, 103, 115
source of beliefs, 33
species, 13, 108, 117
spirit, 98
values, 63
world, 34, 66
humanism, 4, 5, 11, 17, 23, 30, 32–34,
    44, 45, 64, 78, 89, 93, 113, 114
humilation, 8, 115
Hussein, Saddam, 22
hypocrisy, 92, 108

identity, 4, 17, 23, 30, 68–71, 78–80,
    84, 87, 93
    cultural, 15
    religious, 15
    social, 15
ignorance, 1, 22, 53, 60, 71, 74, 108
illness, 33, 48
imagination, 7, 86
imams, 31
immorality, 25
immortality, 109
imperialism, 21, 31, 104, 114

inclusivity, 87
independence, 39, 77, 84, 101
indifference, 31, 96
individualism, 3, 17, 18
individuals, 1, 3, 17, 43, 62, 74, 75,
    93, 102, 104
infancy. *See* childhood
infidels, 18, 20, 31, 70
injustice, 9
insight, 7, 41, 51
integrity, 102, 105
interdependence, 80, 84
intuition, 41, 103
Iraq, 21, 22
Ireland, 2, 31
Islam, 1, 18–20, 22, 25, 27, 112

jihad, 1, 18
Judaism, 18, 26, 27, 32, 112
justice, 45, 104, 105

Kant, Immanuel (1724–1804), 39,
    44, 90
kindness, 98, 107
knowing, 12, 13, 40, 41, 49, 51, 54,
    63, 64, 71, 81, 89
    elision with believing, 46
knowledge, 7, 70. *See also* belief and
    knowledge
    and certainty, 48
    and humility, 49
    and power, 7, 65
    and truth, 13
    basis for, 43
    certain, 38, 62, 77
    creation of, 47, 68
    danger of a little, 38, 40
    duplicity of, 46
    finite, 72
    human, 41, 84
    personal, 8, 40, 59, 73, 79, 109
    revelation of, 7, 38
    scientific, 33, 38, 53, 59, 61–63,
        65, 84
    search for, 69
    threatening, 70

total, 8
ultimate source of, 62
unification of, 62
universal, 12, 68
value of, 108

language, 27, 40, 55, 58, 59, 68, 74,
    77–79, 81, 84, 99, 118
learning, 62, 108
literacy, 103
literature, 5, 78, 84
loneliness, 2, 5, 60, 91
longevity, 56, 70
love, 45, 89, 93, 106, 107

manipulation, 102
martyrdom, 19, 20, 43, 85
mathematics, 40
meaning, 4, 8, 11, 17, 23, 38, 42, 44,
    48, 65, 66, 72, 76, 78, 79, 83, 85, 86,
    110–112
    acceptance of, 21
    and narratives, 84
    and trust, 96
    breakdown of, 44
    changes in, 22, 79, 80
    construction of, 63
    cosmic, 52, 71
    creation of, 45, 47
    defensive, 87
    evidence of, 16
    external, 3, 12, 43, 84
    final, 8
    human, 46
    ideosyncratic, 44
    importance of, 93
    invention of, 8, 12, 42, 84
    loss of, 3, 37, 51, 60, 72, 85, 90
    need for, 4, 23, 86
    of experiences, 16
    of life, 2, 6, 16, 34, 38, 40, 43–45,
        55, 61, 63, 65, 66, 82, 86, 90,
        113, 117
    of universe, 45
    personal, 8, 12, 21, 45, 48, 59, 63,
        67, 68, 82, 84, 91, 100, 111

polarised, 87
ready-made, 61
religious, 73
responsibility for, 91
search for, 69
sense of, 5, 59, 67, 84, 100
shattering of, 18
sources of, 4, 6, 14, 17, 21, 34, 43,
    45, 47, 62, 68, 74, 84
systems, 68
ultimate, 45
meaningfulness, 2, 47, 53, 75
meaninglessness, 12, 21, 44, 45, 60,
    61, 94. *See also* meaning, loss of
media, 15
metanarratives, 47, 74, 81, 92, 93,
    103, 108–10, 112, 114
metaphysics, 12, 37, 43, 44, 53, 59,
    62, 63, 82–84, 90, 92, 110
    as validation of human
        knowledge, 83
    belief in, 83
Methodist Church, 21
mission statements, 17, 105
Mombasa, 2
monism, 42, 58
morality, 2, 5, 12, 13, 17, 19, 20, 43,
    45, 46, 58, 65, 66, 73, 93, 96, 97,
    103, 108, 113–15
mortality, 60, 75, 109
Moscow, 2
Myth of Sisyphus, 42
myths, 4, 8, 15, 38, 80. *See also* beliefs
    and myths

narcissism, 19, 20, 43
narratives, 8, 15, 16, 79, 80, 81, 84,
    110, 111, 114
nationalism, 106
Nietzsche, Friedrich Wilhelm
    (1844–1900), 12, 13, 37, 45, 46, 94,
    109, 118
nihilism, 4, 11, 12, 14, 21, 37, 38,
    43–45, 47, 51, 52, 57, 68, 81–83,
    85, 90, 100, 117
nirvana, 113

noumena, 39

Ockham, William of (1285–1347),
    47
ontology, 60, 112
opportunity, 11, 17, 97, 98
optimism, 63, 65, 95, 98
orthodoxy, 13, 15, 20, 21, 23, 26–29,
    32–35, 42, 44, 46, 47, 49, 65, 66,
    68–70, 87
otherness, 3
Oxford, 24, 107

palaeontology, 52
paranoia, 21, 86
persuasion, 18, 111
phenomena, 39
philosophy, 5, 11–13, 38, 41, 42, 45,
    54, 55, 72, 73, 79, 81, 83, 84, 89, 93,
    95, 114
plurality, 35
    of beliefs, 30
polarisation, 21, 22, 87
politics, 9, 17, 37, 61, 69, 74, 91,
    95–97, 106
Polkinghorne, John, 58, 112–15
postmodernism, 110–11
power, 3, 8, 21, 29, 35, 37, 48, 57, 60,
    61, 69, 74, 89, 93, 104, 111
    and knowledge, 7, 65
pragmatism, 115
priests, 31, 97, 112
progress, 13, 41, 103, 104
public interest, 104
public sector, 104–05
purpose, 2, 3, 12, 13, 16, 23, 38, 43,
    44, 51–53, 60, 65, 66, 72, 82, 95,
    110, 113

quantum physics, 38, 57, 59, 61, 109

rabbis, 26–29, 31
randomness, 53, 56, 58, 71, 75
rationality, 58, 61, 65, 93, 99
reality, 4, 12, 15, 21, 28, 39–41, 58,

60, 62, 63, 65, 69, 75–78, 80, 87, 94, 101, 102, 106, 110–13
reason, 2, 7, 11, 17, 22, 38, 60, 64, 72, 79, 84–86, 110
reasons, 2, 4, 5, 13, 51, 65, 71, 108
reciprocity, 67, 87, 106, 107
reductionism, 100, 112
reflexivity, 78, 101
Reform, 23–26
reincarnation, 82, 109
relationships, 6, 11, 17, 23, 47, 48, 57, 65, 68, 70, 73, 74, 77, 79, 80, 87, 89, 94–97, 102, 104, 106, 107, 111
religion, 2, 11, 17, 18, 26, 27, 31, 43, 47, 53, 62, 65, 69, 70, 82, 86, 87, 97, 98, 106. *See also* beliefs, religious
religious
    attitudes, 23
    books, 28
    community, 2
    conceptions, 51
    creeds, 6, 16, 17
    dialogue, 30
    faith systems, 30
    hunger, 62
    identity, 15
    meaning, 73
    norm, 72
    origins, 31
    orthodoxy, 21, 34, 35, 46, 87
    point of view, 19
    rituals, 16
    scenario, 31
    solution, 71
    studies, 11
    systems, 29
    texts, 17
    understanding, 20, 26
    validity, 11
    values, 95
    war, 18
representation, 78, 79, 97
respect, 4, 23, 32, 42, 66, 83, 85, 87, 91, 92, 96, 98, 105–07, 111
responsibility, 9, 38, 45, 46, 54, 55, 61, 73, 83, 91, 104, 105

retirement, 48
revenge, 19, 22
rhetoric, 97, 105
rights, 9, 104, 105, 111. *See also* human rights
rituals, 16, 17, 31, 45, 80
Rushdie, Salman, 31

Sacks, Jonathan, 15, 26–29, 31, 32, 34, 66, 87, 106
salvation, 13, 19
satire, 102
scepticism, 3, 7, 8, 33, 42, 49, 62, 81, 91–93, 101–04
schism, 25, 32
Schrödinger's cat, 57
science, 7, 33, 34, 38–41, 44, 51, 53, 55, 56, 58, 59, 61–65, 67, 69, 77, 84, 89, 93, 95, 103, 110, 111
    belief in, 59
scientific, 51
    analysis, 34
    certainty, 67
    discoveries, 44, 59
    ethics, 2
    evidence, 66
    experiments, 56
    facts, 5
    knowledge, 33, 53
    reductionism, 112
    sources, 51
    testing, 62
    theory, 13
    thinking, 47
    understanding, 8, 39, 44
scientism, 34, 65
scriptures, 5, 23–25, 29, 31, 32
scrutiny, 33, 42, 78, 92, 103
self, 42, 74, 78, 81, 83, 85, 92, 93, 102, 110, 112
    awareness, 100
    belief, 13, 55
    changes in, 80
    concepts, 18
    dependence on God, 82
    interest, 19

perception, 102
    sense of, 16, 71, 74, 77–79, 84. *See also* subjectivity
significance, 6, 8, 17, 38, 54, 63, 77, 89, 90, 111, 112
    of beliefs, 43
sin, 13, 28, 33
Sisyphus, 42
sleep, 48, 80
social artefacts, 84
social identity, 15
social values, 61
society, 2, 3, 5, 17, 18, 31, 44, 86, 91, 95, 97, 104
solipsism, 82
soul, 13, 58
spirituality, 3, 11, 13, 27, 60, 72, 90, 108, 110
stability, 59
stardust, 57, 58
stem cell, 66
stories, 3, 4, 15, 23, 38
string theory, 57
subjectivity, 30, 47, 67–71, 74–76, 78–82, 100. *See also* self, sense of
suicide, 18, 19, 42, 43, 85
symbols, 4, 15, 40–42, 84
    and beliefs, 42
systems, 105. *See also* belief systems; religious systems; value systems
    immune, 56
    legal, 74
    physical, 77
    political, 74

teleology, 43, 52, 53, 72, 82
television, 1, 17, 48
terror, 19
    war on, 20
terrorism, 18, 20, 43
    September 11, 1, 18, 22, 23, 30, 98
theology, 12, 13, 19, 23, 24, 30, 38, 43, 47, 49, 53, 70, 78, 82, 83, 92, 110, 112
    negative, 44
tolerance, 20, 27, 29, 30, 70, 92, 103

torture, 8, 66, 105, 109
totalitarianism, 65, 103
transparency, 98
trauma, 16, 18, 112
trust, 6, 48, 58, 67, 96, 98, 105, 107
    and meaning, 96
truth, 8, 13, 15, 25–30, 32, 33, 35, 37–39, 46, 47, 62, 69, 70, 76, 106, 111

UK, 11
understanding, 6–8, 13, 16, 20, 26, 38–40, 43–45, 47, 51, 54, 57, 59, 60, 63, 80, 93, 98, 100, 112
United Nations, 22
United States of America, 18, 20, 21, 86
universalism, 30, 84
universe, 5, 12, 41, 43, 45, 57–60, 65, 94, 96, 110–12
unknowability, 39, 77, 78, 112
upheaval, 16

validation, 22, 23, 33, 47, 67, 69, 83, 84, 90
validity, 7, 11, 12, 21, 29, 30, 32, 33, 39, 42, 47, 53, 66, 67, 69, 71, 72, 74, 87, 90, 92–94, 97, 102, 103
    of beliefs, 39, 42
value(s), 2, 4, 7, 9, 44–46, 53, 62, 80, 90, 92, 94–96, 111, 112, 114, 117. *See also* belief and values
    absolute, 60
    and confidence, 66
    and meaning, 63, 83
    and subjectivity, 67
    and the self, 93
    application of, 67
    as escape, 21
    benefit of, 67
    changing, 90, 112
    choice of, 73
    civilised, 20, 22
    create narratives, 111
    façade of, 51
    judgements, 95

knowledge of, 63
loss of, 94
moral, 73
need for, 82, 112
normative, 72
objectivity of, 85
of beliefs, 43
of life, 37, 43, 44
of the other, 20
personal, 4, 5, 9, 12, 14, 33, 54, 83, 87, 89–96, 98, 101, 105, 108, 110–12, 114
political, 61
questions of, 38
responsibility for, 45
revelation of, 7
scientific, 7
sense of, 54, 91
seriousness of, 83
source of, 43–45, 62, 90, 110, 114
statements, 85, 94, 110
systems, 2, 20, 67, 82, 95, 101, 105, 111, 113
validity of, 12
versus fact, 7, 34, 58, 84

versus truth, 39, 70
vengeance, 19
vertigo, 52, 75
vocabulary, 77

Wales, 23, 24
war, 1, 18, 21, 22, 67, 98
on terror, 20
wellbeing, 91, 92, 96, 97, 104
western
life style, 105
metanarratives, 103, 109
philosophy, 30, 74
point of view, 1
sense of the autonomous, 103
sense of time, 109
understanding, 45
wholeness, 100
Williams, Rowan, 4, 22–26, 31, 32, 78, 83, 104. *See also* Canterbury, Archbishop of
witches, 86
Wittgenstein, Ludwig Josef Johann (1889–1951), 43, 49, 81, 83
worship, 31, 113, 118